PYTHON PROGRAMMING FOR RASPBERRY PI

Crafting Innovation Through Code and Hardware

MAXWELL RIVERS

INTRODUCTION

Welcome to 'Python Programming for Raspberry Pi: Crafting Innovation Through Code and Hardware.' This book is all about exploring the exciting world where coding and technology come together. Imagine using a special kind of computer called Raspberry Pi and a super cool programming language called Python to create amazing things!

Think of Python like a set of instructions that tell the computer what to do. And Raspberry Pi is like a tiny computer that you can connect to all sorts of interesting things like lights, buttons, and sensors. When you combine Python and Raspberry Pi, you can make these things do really cool stuff!

In this book, you'll learn the basics of Python and how to use it with Raspberry Pi. You'll learn how to connect things, control them using code, and even make your own projects. Whether you're new to coding or already know a bit, this book will guide you on an adventure of learning and creating.

As you read, you'll discover how to make your own apps, gadgets, and even simple robots! And along the way, you'll find tips to avoid common mistakes and make your code work better. 'Python Programming for Raspberry Pi' is your ticket to a world where your ideas can turn into something amazing. Let's get started!

CONTENTS

INTRODUCTION TO PYTHON AND RASPBERRY PI

Imagine you have a little computer that's as small as a credit card. That's the Raspberry Pi! It's like a tiny brain that can do lots of smart things. Now, think about a language that's really easy to understand, like talking to a friend. That's Python! When you put these two together, you can create all sorts of cool stuff.

Why Python is a Great Choice for Raspberry Pi

Python and the Raspberry Pi are like a dynamic duo in the world of programming and computing.

Simplicity and Readability

Python is known for its simplicity and readability. Instead of complicated symbols and jargon, Python uses words and phrases that are easy to understand, almost like talking in plain English. This makes it a perfect starting point for beginners who are new to programming. When you write code in Python, it's like you're writing instructions for the Raspberry Pi in a language that's straightforward and approachable.

Versatility and Power

The Raspberry Pi might be small, but it's a powerhouse. It's a credit-card-sized computer that can do many things your regular computer can do. It's not limited to just one task – you can use it for everything from playing games to building robots. The Raspberry Pi has the ability to connect to various hardware components like screens, cameras, and sensors, making it a versatile tool for various projects.

A Natural Partnership

Python and the Raspberry Pi go together like peanut butter and jelly. Python's easy-to-understand syntax fits perfectly with the Raspberry Pi's capabilities. With Python, you can tell the Raspberry Pi what to do using commands that make sense. You can control LEDs, take pictures, collect data from sensors, and more, all by writing code in Python. This partnership makes it accessible for newcomers to jump into programming without feeling overwhelmed.

Creativity Unleashed

When you combine Python with the Raspberry Pi, you unlock a world of creativity. You can start small by creating simple programs, and gradually build up to more complex projects. From making games and interactive stories to designing home automation systems and smart devices, Python on the Raspberry Pi lets you bring your ideas to life.

Supportive Community

Both Python and the Raspberry Pi have active and friendly communities that are always ready to help. If you have questions, face challenges, or want to share your creations, you can easily find assistance and inspiration online. This supportive environment makes learning and experimenting even more enjoyable.

Python and the Raspberry Pi are a match made in coding heaven. Python's simplicity and the Raspberry Pi's versatility create an environment where you can learn, experiment, and create without barriers. Whether you're a beginner taking your first steps into programming or an enthusiast dreaming up ambitious projects, the combination of Python and the Raspberry Pi is your ticket to a world of endless possibilities.

Overview of Raspberry Pi and Its Capabilities

Imagine having a computer that fits in your hand and has the power to do some really cool things. That's what the Raspberry Pi is all about!

What is a Raspberry Pi?

The Raspberry Pi is a tiny computer, but don't let its size fool you. It's a mini-computer that's packed with features and possibilities. It's named after the delicious fruit because it's small and sweet, just like the real thing.

A Mini Computer with a Big Heart

Even though the Raspberry Pi is small, it's a complete computer. It has a processor, memory, and storage, just like the computer you might use every day. But what's really exciting is that you can plug in all sorts of things to make it even smarter.

Connecting the World to Your Raspberry Pi

One of the coolest things about the Raspberry Pi is that it's not alone. It has pins sticking out, just like the connectors on your favorite toys. These pins let you attach all sorts of things like buttons, sensors, lights, and even cameras. This means your Raspberry Pi can interact with the world around it.

Different Flavors of Raspberry Pi

Just like there are different flavors of ice cream, there are different types of Raspberry Pi. Each one has its own set of features and abilities. Some are super tiny and great for simple projects, while others are more powerful and can handle bigger tasks. This variety means you can pick the Raspberry Pi that's just right for what you want to do.

What Can You Do with a Raspberry Pi?

The question should be: what can't you do with a Raspberry Pi? You can use it to learn how computers work, play games, make music, create art, build robots, and even make your own gadgets. It's like a toolbox filled with electronic parts that you can use to invent all sorts of cool things.

The Raspberry Pi might be small, but it's a world of possibilities waiting to be explored. Whether you're a beginner who's curious about computers or an experienced maker looking for a new challenge, the Raspberry Pi is your companion on the journey of creativity and discovery. With its versatility and capabilities, you're only limited by your imagination in what you can achieve with this amazing little computer.

Setting Up Your Raspberry Pi for Python Development

Getting started with Python on your Raspberry Pi is like preparing a playground for exciting adventures. Let's walk through the steps to set up your Raspberry Pi so you can dive into the world of Python programming.

Choosing the Right Raspberry Pi

Just like picking the right tool for a job, you'll want to choose the right Raspberry Pi for your needs. There are different models with various features. Some are super small, while others are more powerful. Think about what you want to do and pick the Raspberry Pi that suits your plans.

Gathering the Essentials

Before you start, gather the essentials. You'll need a few things like a keyboard, a mouse, and a monitor to connect to your Raspberry Pi. Don't forget the microSD card, which is like a tiny brain for your Raspberry Pi. It holds the operating system that makes everything work.

Setting Up the Operating System

Just like your computer needs an operating system to work, so does your Raspberry Pi. You'll need to install an operating system on the microSD card. There are different operating systems to choose from, but Raspbian (now known as Raspberry Pi OS) is a popular choice for beginners. It's like the software that runs your Raspberry Pi.

Powering Up and Connecting

Once you've set up the microSD card, insert it into your Raspberry Pi. Connect the keyboard, mouse, and monitor. Then, plug in the power supply to start up your Raspberry Pi. You'll see the operating system's desktop on your monitor, like your Raspberry Pi waking up from a nap.

Meeting the Command Line and Desktop

When your Raspberry Pi is up and running, you can interact with it in two main ways: the command line and the desktop. The command line is like a text-based interface where you type commands, while the desktop is a graphical environment you're probably more familiar with. Both are handy for different tasks.

Installing Python

Python is your key to unlocking the magic of programming on the Raspberry Pi. Fortunately, Python often comes pre-installed on Raspberry Pi OS. You can check by opening a terminal (that's a fancy word for a command line window) and typing **python** or **python3**. If Python isn't installed, you can easily get it using the package manager.

Creating a Virtual Environment

Virtual environments are like separate sandboxes where you can play with Python. They help keep your projects tidy and organized. You can create a virtual environment using the **venv** module. This way, each of your projects can have its own space to grow.

Setting up your Raspberry Pi for Python development is like creating a comfortable workspace for your imagination to run wild. With the right hardware, software, and a touch of curiosity, you've got everything you need to start your journey into Python programming on the Raspberry Pi. From here, you're ready to start writing code, experimenting, and bringing your ideas to life.

PYTHON BASICS

Installing Python on Raspberry Pi

Python is like the paintbrush and Raspberry Pi is the canvas – together, they let you create amazing things. To start this creative journey, let's learn how to bring Python to your Raspberry Pi.

Checking if Python is Already Installed

Before you dive into installation, it's good to check if Python is already hanging out on your Raspberry Pi. Open a terminal, which is like a chat window with your Raspberry Pi, and type **python3 --version**. If you get a response showing a version number, great! You're all set. If not, don't worry – we'll install it.

Updating Your System

It's a good idea to make sure your Raspberry Pi is up-to-date before installing Python. In the same terminal, type:

```
sudo apt update
sudo apt upgrade
```

This makes sure your Raspberry Pi knows about all the latest stuff.

Installing Python

Now comes the exciting part: installing Python. You'll use a package manager, which is like a friendly delivery service for software. In the terminal, type:

```
sudo apt install python3
```

This tells your Raspberry Pi to fetch and install Python for you. It might ask for your password – that's normal. Once it's done, you're ready to go!

Checking Python's Installation

To double-check that Python is installed, you can run:

```
python3 --version
```

You should see the version number show up. Now you have Python on your Raspberry Pi, like having your favorite color of paint ready to use.

Pip: Your Python Companion

Python comes with a friend called **pip**, which stands for "Python Package Installer." It's like a tool that helps you easily add extra stuff to Python. To make sure it's there, type:

```
pip3 --version
```

If it's not installed, you can install it by typing:

```
sudo apt install python3-pip
```

With Python installed on your Raspberry Pi, you've unlocked a world of possibilities. It's like having a magic wand that lets you command your Raspberry Pi to do incredible things. Now that you're all set up, it's time to start writing your first lines of code and exploring the wonderful world of Python programming on your Raspberry Pi.

Python Syntax and Structure

Imagine Python as a special language that lets you communicate with computers. But just like any language, it has rules and patterns. These rules make up the syntax, and the way you organize your code is its structure.

Hello, Python!

In Python, you communicate with the computer by writing lines of code. Each line is like a sentence that tells the computer what to do. For example, let's say you want the computer to say "Hello, World!" This is how you'd do it:

```
print("Hello, World!")
```

The **print()** function is like a messenger that tells the computer to display something. In Python, you often use parentheses **()** to tell functions what to do.

Indentation: Python's Quirk

Python has a unique feature: it cares a lot about how you organize your code visually. Other programming languages use symbols like { and } to group code, but Python uses indentation. This means you need to be careful with spaces or tabs at the beginning of lines.

For example, when defining a loop, the indentation shows which lines are part of the loop:

```
for i in range(5):
    print(i)
```

Variables: Names for Your Stuff

Variables are like labeled boxes that hold stuff. You can give a name to a variable and then use that name to access what's inside. Think of it like labeling a lunchbox with your name – when you want your lunch, you just look for your name.

```
name = "Alice"
age = 25
print(name)
print(age)
```

Comments: Notes for Humans

Sometimes you want to explain what your code does. That's where comments come in. Comments are notes you write for yourself (and others) that don't affect how the computer runs the code.

```
# This is a comment. The computer ignores it.
print("Hello, Python!")
```

Python's syntax and structure are like the grammar and structure of a language. Once you understand the rules, you can start writing meaningful code that the computer understands. Remember to be precise with your punctuation (like parentheses) and careful with your indentation. As you explore further, you'll discover how to combine these building blocks to create amazing programs and bring your ideas to life!

Variables, Data Types, and Basic Operations in Python

In the world of programming, you often need to store information and perform operations on it. This is where variables and data types come into play.

Variables: Containers of Information

Variables are like labeled boxes where you can store different types of information. Each variable has a name, and you can use that name to access the data stored inside. Think of them as containers that hold values you can use later.

```
name = "Alice"
age = 25
```

In this example, **name** and **age** are variables. **name** holds the text "Alice," and **age** holds the number 25.

Data Types: Categories of Information

Every piece of information in Python belongs to a data type. There are different types for different kinds of data. The main data types include:

- **Strings**: Textual data, like words and sentences.
- **Integers**: Whole numbers.
- **Floats**: Decimal numbers.
- **Booleans**: Values that are either **True** or **False**.

Python automatically figures out the data type based on what you put in a variable.

Basic Operations: Playing with Data

You can perform various operations on data using operators. Here are some basic ones:

- **Arithmetic Operators**: Used for mathematical calculations.

```
x = 10
y = 5
sum_result = x + y  # Addition
diff_result = x - y  # Subtraction
prod_result = x * y  # Multiplication
div_result = x / y   # Division
```

- **Concatenation**: Used to combine strings.

```
first_name = "John"
last_name = "Doe"
full_name = first_name + " " + last_name
```

- **Comparison Operators**: Used to compare values.

```
x = 10
y = 5
is_equal = x == y    # Equal to
```

```
is_not_equal = x != y # Not equal to
is_greater = x > y   # Greater than
is_less = x < y      # Less than
```

- **Boolean Operators**: Used to combine conditions.

```
is_adult = age >= 18  # Greater than or equal to
is_student = True
can_enter = is_adult and not is_student  # Logical AND and NOT
```

Variables, data types, and basic operations are the building blocks of programming. They allow you to store information, manipulate it, and make decisions based on it. By understanding how to use these concepts, you're well on your way to creating more complex programs and solving real-world problems using Python.

Control Structures: If Statements, Loops, and More

In the world of programming, you don't just tell the computer what to do once; you often need to make decisions and repeat actions. This is where control structures come in. They let you guide the flow of your program and make it more dynamic.

If Statements: Making Decisions

If statements are like forks in the road. They let your program decide which path to take based on certain conditions. Imagine you're deciding whether to take an umbrella outside – if it's raining, you'll grab the umbrella; if it's not, you'll leave it behind.

```
weather = "rainy"
```

```
if weather == "rainy":
    print("Take an umbrella!")
else:
    print("No need for an umbrella.")
```

In this example, if the **weather** is "rainy," the program takes one path; if it's not, it takes the other.

Loops: Repeating Actions

Loops are like repeat buttons for your code. They allow you to perform the same actions multiple times. Imagine you're writing a thank-you note to many friends – instead of writing the same thing over and over, you'd use a loop.

While Loop:

```
count = 1
while count <= 5:
    print("Thank you!")
    count += 1
```

For Loop:

```
fruits = ["apple", "banana", "orange"]
for fruit in fruits:
    print("I love", fruit)
```

In the while loop, the code keeps saying "Thank you!" as long as **count** is less than or equal to 5. In the for loop, the code goes through each fruit in the list and says "I love" along with the fruit's name.

Nested Control Structures: Building Complexity

You can also put control structures inside each other. This lets you create more intricate patterns of decision-making and repetition. It's like having a decision within a decision, or a loop inside a loop.

Combining Control Structures

Often, you'll use a combination of if statements and loops to create dynamic programs. You might check a condition, then loop through some actions, and check another condition – all to achieve a particular outcome.

Control structures are the choreography of your program. They let you make decisions, repeat actions, and create complex patterns of behavior. By mastering if statements, loops, and the art of combining them, you can create programs that adapt, respond, and accomplish tasks in ways that were once just an idea in your mind.

Functions and Modular Programming in Python

Imagine you're baking a cake. You follow a recipe that tells you what ingredients to use and how to mix them. Now, imagine you could put parts of that recipe into separate reusable cards. That's what functions do in programming. They let you create efficient, organized, and reusable pieces of code.

What Are Functions?

Functions are like mini-programs within your main program. They group together a set of instructions that you can use again and again with different inputs. Just like a recipe card for baking, a function contains a series of steps that perform a specific task.

Creating a Function

In Python, you create a function using the **def** keyword. Let's say you want a function to greet someone:

```
def greet(name):
    print("Hello,", name)
```

Here, **greet** is the name of the function, and **name** is a parameter – the input it needs to do its job.

Using a Function

Once you've defined a function, you can use it by "calling" it. Calling a function is like using that recipe card you made earlier.

```
greet("Alice")
greet("Bob")
```

When you call **greet("Alice")**, the function executes its steps with "Alice" as the input for **name**.

Return Values

Functions can also give you something back after they've done their job. Imagine your cake recipe card not only tells you the steps but also the delicious cake you made. In programming, this is called the "return value."

```
def add(x, y):
    return x + y

result = add(3, 5)
print(result)  # Outputs: 8
```

Modular Programming: Building with Blocks

Modular programming is like building with Lego blocks. Instead of making a huge sculpture in one go, you create smaller pieces (functions) that fit together seamlessly. This makes your code cleaner, easier to understand, and simpler to maintain.

Benefits of Functions and Modular Programming

- **Reuse**: You write the code once and use it as many times as needed.

- **Organization**: Code is divided into logical blocks, making it easier to manage.

- **Readability**: Functions give meaningful names to tasks, making your code more understandable.

- **Debugging**: If something goes wrong, you can focus on a single function, making it easier to find and fix issues.

Functions and modular programming are like the tools that help you build a complex structure piece by piece. They make your code cleaner, more efficient, and easier to manage. By using functions, you can create a library of building blocks that you can assemble to create powerful and dynamic programs in Python.

WORKING WITH GPIO (GENERAL PURPOSE INPUT OUTPUT)

Understanding GPIO Pins on Raspberry Pi

Imagine your Raspberry Pi is like a playground where you can connect and control different electronic devices. GPIO (General Purpose Input Output) pins are the gateways that allow your Raspberry Pi to interact with the physical world.

What are GPIO Pins?

GPIO pins are like tiny electronic switches on your Raspberry Pi. They can be used to send or receive electrical signals to and from external devices like sensors, LEDs, buttons, motors, and more. These pins can be programmed to be either inputs or outputs, giving you the ability to control and communicate with various components.

Numbering and Layout

Raspberry Pi boards have a specific layout of GPIO pins. They are usually labeled with numbers, making it easy to identify and work with each pin. There are different models of Raspberry Pi, and they might have varying numbers of GPIO pins, but the concept remains the same.

Using GPIO Pins as Outputs

When you set a GPIO pin as an output, you can use it to control external components like LEDs or motors. For example, you can make an LED blink by turning the GPIO pin on and off at specific intervals.

```python
import RPi.GPIO as GPIO
import time

GPIO.setmode(GPIO.BOARD)
led_pin = 11

GPIO.setup(led_pin, GPIO.OUT)

while True:
    GPIO.output(led_pin, GPIO.HIGH)  # Turn LED on
    time.sleep(1)
    GPIO.output(led_pin, GPIO.LOW)   # Turn LED off
    time.sleep(1)

GPIO.cleanup()
```

In this example, the GPIO pin with number 11 is used to control an LED. The code turns the LED on for a second, then turns it off for a second, creating a blinking effect.

Using GPIO Pins as Inputs

When you set a GPIO pin as an input, you can read the state of external components like buttons or sensors. For example, you can create a program that reacts to a button press.

```
import RPi.GPIO as GPIO

GPIO.setmode(GPIO.BOARD)
button_pin = 13

GPIO.setup(button_pin, GPIO.IN,
pull_up_down=GPIO.PUD_DOWN)

while True:
    if GPIO.input(button_pin) == GPIO.HIGH:
        print("Button pressed!")

GPIO.cleanup()
```

Here, the code reads the state of the GPIO pin with number 13, which is connected to a button. When the button is pressed, the code detects a high signal and prints "Button pressed!"

GPIO pins turn your Raspberry Pi into a versatile controller that can interact with the physical world. Whether you're lighting up LEDs, reading sensor data, or controlling motors, GPIO pins are the bridge between your code and the real world, allowing you to bring your creative ideas to life.

Configuring GPIO Pins Using Python

Configuring GPIO pins with Python on your Raspberry Pi is like giving your computer a secret handshake to communicate with the outside world. By understanding how to set up and control GPIO pins, you'll have the power to build interactive projects that respond to your commands.

Setting Up GPIO Pins

To start using GPIO pins, you'll need to import the **RPi.GPIO** module. If you haven't installed it, you can do so using the command **pip install RPi.GPIO**.

```
import RPi.GPIO as GPIO
```

Next, you need to set the numbering mode for GPIO pins. There are two modes: **GPIO.BCM** and **GPIO.BOARD**.

- **GPIO.BCM**: Uses the Broadcom SOC channel numbers, which are often referred to as GPIOxx, where xx is the channel number.
- **GPIO.BOARD**: Uses the physical pin numbers as they are labeled on the Raspberry Pi.

```
GPIO.setmode(GPIO.BCM)
```

Configuring Pins as Inputs or Outputs

Before you use a GPIO pin, you must configure it as an input or an output. For example, to set up pin 17 as an output:

```
led_pin = 17
GPIO.setup(led_pin, GPIO.OUT)
```

And to set up pin 22 as an input with a pull-down resistor:

```
button_pin = 22
GPIO.setup(button_pin, GPIO.IN,
```

```
pull_up_down=GPIO.PUD_DOWN)
```

Controlling Output Pins

Once a pin is set up as an output, you can control it by turning it on or off. For example, to turn on an LED connected to pin 17:

```
GPIO.output(led_pin, GPIO.HIGH) # Turn on
```

And to turn it off:

```
GPIO.output(led_pin, GPIO.LOW)  # Turn off
```

Reading Input Pins

When a pin is configured as an input, you can read its state. For instance, to check if a button connected to pin 22 is pressed:

```
if GPIO.input(button_pin) == GPIO.HIGH:
    print("Button pressed!")
```

Cleaning Up

After you're done using GPIO pins, it's important to clean up to avoid conflicts in the future.

```
GPIO.cleanup()
```

Putting It All Together

Here's a simple example that blinks an LED when a button is pressed:

```
import RPi.GPIO as GPIO
import time

GPIO.setmode(GPIO.BCM)
led_pin = 17
button_pin = 22

GPIO.setup(led_pin, GPIO.OUT)
GPIO.setup(button_pin, GPIO.IN,
pull_up_down=GPIO.PUD_DOWN)

while True:
  if GPIO.input(button_pin) == GPIO.HIGH:
    GPIO.output(led_pin, GPIO.HIGH)
  else:
    GPIO.output(led_pin, GPIO.LOW)

GPIO.cleanup()
```

Configuring GPIO pins using Python allows you to interact with external components, turning your Raspberry Pi into a versatile tool for creating interactive projects. Whether you're controlling LEDs, reading sensors, or interacting with buttons, understanding how to configure and control GPIO pins opens the door to a world of creative possibilities.

Reading Input from Sensors and Buttons

Sensors and buttons are like the eyes and ears of your electronic projects. They help your Raspberry Pi gather information from the environment and respond accordingly.

Connecting Sensors and Buttons

Before you can read input from sensors and buttons, you need to connect them to your Raspberry Pi's GPIO pins. Make sure to follow the datasheet or instructions for the specific sensor or button you're using. For example, a simple button might have one leg connected to a GPIO pin and the other to a ground pin, creating a simple circuit.

Reading Buttons

Buttons are like digital switches – they're either pressed (closed) or not pressed (open). You can use the GPIO input function to read the state of a button.

```python
import RPi.GPIO as GPIO

GPIO.setmode(GPIO.BCM)
button_pin = 17

GPIO.setup(button_pin, GPIO.IN,
pull_up_down=GPIO.PUD_DOWN)

while True:
    if GPIO.input(button_pin) == GPIO.HIGH:
        print("Button pressed!")
```

In this example, when the button connected to pin 17 is pressed, the program prints "Button pressed!".

Reading Sensors

Sensors provide analog or digital data that you can use to measure various environmental factors. For analog sensors, you'll need to use an analog-to-digital converter (ADC) to read their values.

Here's an example using a digital temperature and humidity sensor (DHT11) that outputs data digitally:

```
import RPi.GPIO as GPIO
import dht11

GPIO.setmode(GPIO.BCM)
dht_pin = 18

instance = dht11.DHT11(pin=dht_pin)

while True:
    result = instance.read()
    if result.is_valid():
        print(f"Temperature: {result.temperature}°C, Humidity:
{result.humidity}%")
```

In this example, the DHT11 sensor connected to pin 18 provides temperature and humidity data.

Debouncing Buttons

Buttons can sometimes generate noisy signals when pressed due to physical bouncing. To avoid this, you can implement software debouncing by adding a delay.

```
import RPi.GPIO as GPIO
import time

GPIO.setmode(GPIO.BCM)
button_pin = 17

GPIO.setup(button_pin, GPIO.IN,
pull_up_down=GPIO.PUD_DOWN)

while True:
    if GPIO.input(button_pin) == GPIO.HIGH:
        print("Button pressed!")
        time.sleep(0.2)  # Debounce delay
```

Reading input from sensors and buttons adds a new dimension to your Raspberry Pi projects. Whether you're detecting environmental changes, responding to user input, or creating interactive experiences, understanding how to read and interpret sensor and button data using Python opens up a world of creative possibilities.

Controlling LEDs and Other Output Devices

Controlling output devices like LEDs, motors, and displays using your Raspberry Pi adds the element of interaction and visual feedback to your projects. With Python, you can easily command these devices to light up, spin, or display information.

Connecting and Configuring LEDs

Before you can control LEDs, you need to connect them to GPIO pins on your Raspberry Pi. Connect the longer leg (anode) of the LED to a GPIO pin and the shorter leg (cathode) to a ground pin. To control the LED, configure the GPIO pin as an output and toggle its state between high and low.

```
import RPi.GPIO as GPIO
import time

GPIO.setmode(GPIO.BCM)
led_pin = 17

GPIO.setup(led_pin, GPIO.OUT)

while True:
  GPIO.output(led_pin, GPIO.HIGH)  # Turn on the LED
  time.sleep(1)
  GPIO.output(led_pin, GPIO.LOW)   # Turn off the LED
```

```
time.sleep(1)
```

This code turns on the LED connected to pin 17 for one second, then turns it off for one second, creating a blinking effect.

Controlling Motors

To control motors, you often need additional components like motor drivers. These drivers provide the necessary power and control signals to make the motor spin. While the exact setup can vary based on the motor and driver you're using, the concept remains similar – you'll use GPIO pins to send control signals to the motor driver.

```
import RPi.GPIO as GPIO
import time

GPIO.setmode(GPIO.BCM)
motor_pin = 18

GPIO.setup(motor_pin, GPIO.OUT)

motor_pwm = GPIO.PWM(motor_pin, 1000)  # Create a PWM
object
motor_pwm.start(50)  # Start the motor at 50% speed

time.sleep(3)  # Run the motor for 3 seconds

motor_pwm.stop()  # Stop the motor
GPIO.cleanup()
```

This example uses a pulse-width modulation (PWM) signal to control the speed of a motor connected to pin 18. The motor runs at 50% speed for 3 seconds.

Displaying Information on a LED Matrix

LED matrices are arrays of LEDs that can display patterns or messages. To control them, you'll need additional libraries like **rpi_ws281x**. Here's a basic example using a single LED from an LED matrix:

```python
import time
from rpi_ws281x import PixelStrip, Color

LED_COUNT = 1
LED_PIN = 18

strip = PixelStrip(LED_COUNT, LED_PIN)
strip.begin()

strip.setPixelColor(0, Color(255, 0, 0))  # Set the color of the first
LED to red
strip.show()

time.sleep(2)

strip.setPixelColor(0, Color(0, 255, 0))  # Change the color to
green
strip.show()

strip.setPixelColor(0, Color(0, 0, 255))  # Change the color to blue
strip.show()

strip.setPixelColor(0, Color(0, 0, 0))    # Turn off the LED
strip.show()
```

This example sets the color of a single LED to red, then green, then blue, and finally turns it off.

Controlling LEDs, motors, and other output devices with Python and your Raspberry Pi lets you add movement, light, and visual information to your projects. Whether you're building displays, animations, or interactive devices, mastering the art of controlling output devices allows you to create projects that engage and captivate your audience.

PWM (Pulse Width Modulation) for Analog-like Output

Imagine having a magical dimmer switch for your LEDs or a precise speed control for your motors. That's what PWM (Pulse Width Modulation) brings to your Raspberry Pi projects. PWM allows you to simulate analog-like outputs by rapidly toggling a digital signal on and off.

Understanding PWM

PWM is a technique where you control the average voltage or power delivered to a device by varying the width of the pulses in a digital signal. When you want to create an effect like dimming an LED, instead of continuously decreasing the voltage (which is what analog dimmers do), PWM rapidly switches the LED on and off. By varying the ratio of the on-time to the off-time, you achieve the illusion of dimming.

Using PWM in Python

To use PWM with Python on a Raspberry Pi, you can utilize the **RPi.GPIO** library. This library provides functions to create PWM signals on compatible GPIO pins. Here's an example of controlling the brightness of an LED using PWM:

```
import RPi.GPIO as GPIO
```

```
import time

GPIO.setmode(GPIO.BCM)
led_pin = 18

GPIO.setup(led_pin, GPIO.OUT)

pwm = GPIO.PWM(led_pin, 100)  # Create a PWM object with a
frequency of 100 Hz
pwm.start(0)  # Start with 0% duty cycle (LED is off)

try:
    while True:
        for duty_cycle in range(0, 101, 5):  # Vary duty cycle from 0
to 100 in steps of 5
            pwm.ChangeDutyCycle(duty_cycle)
            time.sleep(0.1)
        for duty_cycle in range(100, -1, -5):  # Vary duty cycle from
100 to 0 in steps of 5
            pwm.ChangeDutyCycle(duty_cycle)
            time.sleep(0.1)
except KeyboardInterrupt:
    pass

pwm.stop()
GPIO.cleanup()
```

In this example, the PWM signal is generated on pin 18, and the LED connected to it appears to smoothly change its brightness.

Applications of PWM

PWM finds its application in various fields:

- **LED Dimming**: Create fading or pulsing effects for LEDs.
- **Motor Speed Control**: Vary motor speeds in robotics projects.
- **Analog Simulation**: Simulate analog outputs for devices that

accept variable voltage.

- **Audio Generation**: Generate audio tones or signals.
- **Servo Motor Control**: Position servo motors accurately in robotics.

PWM is like having a secret weapon for controlling analog-like behavior with digital signals. By understanding and using PWM in your Raspberry Pi projects, you gain the ability to control a wide range of devices with variable outputs, making your projects more dynamic, versatile, and closer to the real world's behavior.

INTERFACING WITH SENSORS AND ACTUATORS

Introduction to Various Sensors: Temperature, Humidity, Motion, and More

Sensors are like the senses of your electronic projects, allowing your Raspberry Pi to gather information from the environment. These sensors open up a world of possibilities, from monitoring weather conditions to detecting motion and capturing data.

Temperature and Humidity Sensors

Temperature and humidity sensors are often combined into a single module. They provide accurate measurements of the surrounding temperature and relative humidity. One common sensor in this category is the DHT11 or DHT22.

How They Work: These sensors usually consist of a humidity-sensitive element and a temperature-sensitive element. Changes in humidity cause the element to expand or contract, affecting the resistance, which is then converted into humidity values. The temperature-sensitive element works on similar principles.

Usage: Weather stations, indoor climate monitoring, plant growth monitoring, and HVAC systems.

Ultrasonic Distance Sensors

Ultrasonic distance sensors measure distances using sound waves. They emit ultrasonic pulses and measure the time taken for the pulse to bounce back after hitting an object. This time can be used to calculate the distance to the object.

How They Work: The sensor emits ultrasonic waves and waits for them to bounce back. By measuring the time it takes for the waves to return, the sensor calculates the distance using the speed of sound.

Usage: Proximity detection, obstacle avoidance in robotics, liquid level measurement, and security systems.

PIR Motion Sensors

Passive Infrared (PIR) sensors detect changes in infrared radiation, such as those caused by movement. They are commonly used to detect human or animal presence.

How They Work: PIR sensors contain a pyroelectric sensor that can detect changes in infrared radiation. When a warm object (like a person) moves across the sensor's field of view, it generates a change in the infrared radiation pattern, triggering the sensor.

Usage: Intruder detection, occupancy sensing, automatic lighting control, and home automation.

Light Sensors (Photocells)

Light sensors, also known as photocells or light-dependent

resistors (LDRs), measure the intensity of light in their surroundings.

How They Work: LDRs change their resistance based on the amount of light falling on them. More light leads to lower resistance, and less light leads to higher resistance.

Usage: Automatic streetlights, indoor lighting control, photography equipment, and solar-powered devices.

Gas Sensors

Gas sensors are used to detect the presence of specific gases in the environment, like carbon monoxide, methane, or volatile organic compounds (VOCs).

How They Work: Different types of gas sensors work based on various principles, such as catalytic, electrochemical, or semiconductor. They respond to changes in gas concentration by altering their electrical properties.

Usage: Indoor air quality monitoring, gas leak detection, industrial safety, and environmental monitoring.

Sensors are the eyes and ears of your electronic projects, allowing them to interact with the world in meaningful ways. By understanding how different sensors work and how to interface them with your Raspberry Pi using Python, you can gather data, automate tasks, and create projects that respond intelligently to their surroundings.

Reading Sensor Data Using Python

Reading sensor data using Python and your Raspberry Pi opens up a realm of possibilities for collecting, analyzing, and responding to information from the physical world. By mastering the art of reading sensor data, you can create projects that monitor environments, automate processes, and even predict future trends.

Importing Necessary Libraries

Before you start reading sensor data, you'll need to import the appropriate libraries. Different sensors may require specific libraries for communication. For example, the DHT11 temperature and humidity sensor can be interfaced using the **Adafruit_DHT** library.

```
import Adafruit_DHT
```

Reading Temperature and Humidity Data

Let's say you're using a DHT11 sensor to measure temperature and humidity. Here's how you might read data from it:

```
import Adafruit_DHT
import time

sensor = Adafruit_DHT.DHT11
pin = 4  # GPIO pin number

while True:
    humidity, temperature = Adafruit_DHT.read_retry(sensor, pin)
    if humidity is not None and temperature is not None:
        print(f"Temperature: {temperature}°C, Humidity:
{humidity}%")
    else:
        print("Failed to retrieve data")
    time.sleep(2)
```

In this example, the **read_retry()** function attempts to read data from the sensor, and if successful, it prints out the temperature and humidity values.

Reading Distance from Ultrasonic Sensor

Suppose you're using an ultrasonic distance sensor to measure distances. Here's an example using the **gpiozero** library:

```
from gpiozero import DistanceSensor
import time

sensor = DistanceSensor(echo=17, trigger=27)

while True:
    distance = sensor.distance
    print(f"Distance: {distance:.2f} meters")
    time.sleep(2)
```

In this example, the **DistanceSensor** class from **gpiozero** library simplifies the interface to the ultrasonic sensor. The **distance** attribute provides the distance measurement.

Customizing and Using Other Sensors

Different sensors may require different libraries and communication protocols. Always refer to the sensor's datasheet and documentation for guidance on how to interface with it using Python.

Reading sensor data using Python transforms your Raspberry Pi into a data-gathering powerhouse. By interfacing with various sensors and libraries, you can capture real-world information, from temperature and humidity to distance and more. This data can then be used to make informed decisions, automate processes, or even visualize trends. The ability to read sensor data opens up a world of creativity and innovation in your projects.

Using Libraries for Sensor Integration

Integrating sensors into your Raspberry Pi projects becomes much simpler and efficient when you leverage existing libraries. These libraries provide pre-built functions and abstractions that handle low-level communication with sensors, allowing you to focus on using the data rather than dealing with complex hardware interactions.

Why Use Libraries?

1. **Abstraction**: Libraries abstract the low-level details of sensor communication, making it easier to work with sensors.
2. **Time-Saving**: Libraries provide pre-built functions for common tasks, saving you time and effort.
3. **Reliability**: Libraries are usually well-tested and maintained by a community of developers.
4. **Consistency**: Libraries often follow consistent naming conventions and coding patterns, making your code cleaner.

Installing Libraries

To use a library, you typically need to install it first. You can do this using tools like **pip**, the Python package manager. For example, to install the **Adafruit_DHT** library for the DHT11 temperature and humidity sensor:

```
pip install Adafruit_DHT
```

Using Libraries for Sensor Integration

Let's look at how to use the **Adafruit_DHT** library to read data from a DHT11 sensor.

```
import Adafruit_DHT
import time

sensor = Adafruit_DHT.DHT11
pin = 4  # GPIO pin number

while True:
    humidity, temperature = Adafruit_DHT.read_retry(sensor, pin)
    if humidity is not None and temperature is not None:
        print(f"Temperature: {temperature}°C, Humidity:
{humidity}%")
    else:
        print("Failed to retrieve data")
    time.sleep(2)
```

In this example, the **Adafruit_DHT** library abstracts the details of interacting with the DHT11 sensor. The **read_retry()** function handles retries in case of failed readings.

Using gpiozero for Sensors

The **gpiozero** library simplifies sensor integration even further. Here's how you might use it to work with a distance sensor.

```
from gpiozero import DistanceSensor
import time

sensor = DistanceSensor(echo=17, trigger=27)
```

```
while True:
    distance = sensor.distance
    print(f"Distance: {distance:.2f} meters")
    time.sleep(2)
```

The **DistanceSensor** class abstracts the complexities of interfacing with the ultrasonic distance sensor.

Exploring Other Libraries

- **smbus** and **smbus2**: Libraries for I2C communication with sensors.

- **gpiozero**: Provides easy-to-use abstractions for GPIO pins and devices.

- **RPi.GPIO**: Offers tools for working with the Raspberry Pi's GPIO pins.

- **adafruit-circuitpython**: Provides a collection of libraries for various sensors and components.

Using libraries for sensor integration streamlines the process of interfacing with sensors, making your projects more manageable and reducing the barriers to entry for working with hardware. Whether you're reading temperature, detecting motion, measuring distances, or any other task, leveraging libraries allows you to focus on the creative aspects of your projects without getting bogged down in hardware details.

Controlling Servos and Motors

Servos and motors are like the muscles of your electronic projects, enabling motion and mechanical interactions. By controlling servos and motors with your Raspberry Pi, you can bring your creations to life, whether it's a robot arm, a car, or a remotely controlled device.

Servo Motors

Servo motors are widely used for their precise control of angular positions. They're commonly found in robotics and mechanisms that require controlled movement within a specific range.

Using the RPi.GPIO Library

```
import RPi.GPIO as GPIO
import time

GPIO.setmode(GPIO.BCM)
servo_pin = 18

GPIO.setup(servo_pin, GPIO.OUT)

pwm = GPIO.PWM(servo_pin, 50)  # Create a PWM object with a
frequency of 50 Hz
pwm.start(0)  # Start with 0% duty cycle (servo at min position)

try:
    while True:
        for angle in range(0, 181, 10):  # Rotate servo from 0 to 180
degrees in steps of 10
            duty_cycle = (angle / 18) + 2
            pwm.ChangeDutyCycle(duty_cycle)
            time.sleep(0.5)
except KeyboardInterrupt:
    pass

pwm.stop()
GPIO.cleanup()
```

In this example, the servo motor is connected to pin 18. The duty cycle of the PWM signal controls the servo's angle, moving it from 0 to 180 degrees in steps of 10.

DC Motors

DC motors are versatile and commonly used for a wide range of applications, from robotic wheels to conveyor belts.

Using the gpiozero Library

```python
from gpiozero import Motor
import time

motor = Motor(forward=17, backward=18)

while True:
    motor.forward()  # Turn the motor forward
    time.sleep(2)
    motor.backward()  # Turn the motor backward
    time.sleep(2)
    motor.stop()  # Stop the motor
    time.sleep(2)
```

In this example, the **Motor** class from the **gpiozero** library is used to control a DC motor connected to pins 17 and 18. The motor can be moved forward, backward, or stopped.

Stepper Motors

Stepper motors provide precise control of rotational angles and are often used in applications that require accurate positioning, such as 3D printers and CNC machines.

Using the RPi.GPIO Library

```python
import RPi.GPIO as GPIO
import time
```

```
GPIO.setmode(GPIO.BCM)
coil_A_1_pin = 4
coil_A_2_pin = 17
coil_B_1_pin = 23
coil_B_2_pin = 24

GPIO.setup(coil_A_1_pin, GPIO.OUT)
GPIO.setup(coil_A_2_pin, GPIO.OUT)
GPIO.setup(coil_B_1_pin, GPIO.OUT)
GPIO.setup(coil_B_2_pin, GPIO.OUT)

def forward(delay, steps):
   for i in range(steps):
      setStep(1, 0, 1, 0)
      time.sleep(delay)
      setStep(0, 1, 1, 0)
      time.sleep(delay)
      setStep(0, 1, 0, 1)
      time.sleep(delay)
      setStep(1, 0, 0, 1)
      time.sleep(delay)

def setStep(w1, w2, w3, w4):
   GPIO.output(coil_A_1_pin, w1)
   GPIO.output(coil_A_2_pin, w2)
   GPIO.output(coil_B_1_pin, w3)
   GPIO.output(coil_B_2_pin, w4)

try:
   while True:
      delay = 5 / 1000
      steps = 100
      forward(delay, steps)
except KeyboardInterrupt:
   pass

GPIO.cleanup()
```

In this example, the stepper motor is controlled by driving its coils in a specific sequence. The **setStep** function sets the state of each coil, and the **forward** function moves the stepper motor forward.

Controlling servos, DC motors, and stepper motors with Python gives you the ability to create dynamic and interactive projects that move and respond to their environment. Whether it's for robotics, automation, or any other mechanical task, mastering the control of motors allows you to add a new dimension of functionality to your Raspberry Pi projects.

Building Simple Robotics Projects

Robotics projects bring together hardware and software to create intelligent, interactive, and sometimes autonomous systems. With your Raspberry Pi and a few components, you can embark on exciting robotics adventures that range from basic movements to more complex behaviors.

1. Line Following Robot

Concept: Create a robot that can follow a line on the ground using sensors.

Components:
- Raspberry Pi
- Infrared sensors (line sensors)
- Motor driver or H-bridge module
- Wheels and DC motors
- Chassis

Implementation:

1. Attach the line sensors under the robot chassis, facing downwards.

2. Connect the sensors and motors to the Raspberry Pi using the motor driver.

3. Write a program to read sensor data and control the motors to keep the robot on the line.

2. Obstacle Avoidance Robot

Concept: Build a robot that can navigate and avoid obstacles in its path.

Components:

- Raspberry Pi
- Ultrasonic distance sensor
- Motor driver or H-bridge module
- Wheels and DC motors
- Chassis

Implementation:

1. Mount the ultrasonic sensor at the front of the robot.

2. Connect the sensor and motors to the Raspberry Pi using the motor driver.

3. Develop a program that reads the distance from the sensor and maneuvers the robot to avoid obstacles.

3. Remote-Controlled Car

Concept: Create a car that can be controlled remotely using a smartphone or computer.

Components:

- Raspberry Pi

- Motor driver or H-bridge module
- Wheels and DC motors
- Chassis
- Wi-Fi module (Wi-Fi dongle or onboard Wi-Fi)

Implementation:

1. Assemble the car chassis and attach the motors.
2. Connect the motors and Wi-Fi module to the Raspberry Pi using the motor driver.
3. Develop a program that establishes a Wi-Fi connection and listens for control commands from a remote device.

4. Gesture-Controlled Robot

Concept: Build a robot that responds to hand gestures for movement.

Components:

- Raspberry Pi
- Gesture recognition sensor (e.g., accelerometer or gyroscope)
- Motor driver or H-bridge module
- Wheels and DC motors
- Chassis

Implementation:

1. Install the gesture recognition sensor on the robot.
2. Connect the sensor and motors to the Raspberry Pi using the motor driver.
3. Write a program that interprets gestures from the sensor and controls the robot accordingly.

5. Maze-Solving Robot

Concept: Construct a robot that can navigate through a maze and reach the exit.

Components:

- Raspberry Pi
- Infrared sensors (for wall detection)
- Motor driver or H-bridge module
- Wheels and DC motors
- Chassis

Implementation:

1. Attach the infrared sensors to the sides of the robot.
2. Connect the sensors and motors to the Raspberry Pi using the motor driver.
3. Develop an algorithm to navigate the maze by following walls and making decisions at intersections.

Building simple robotics projects with your Raspberry Pi introduces you to the exciting world of robotics, programming, and electronics. These projects serve as a starting point, allowing you to explore and expand your skills in robotics and automation. As you become more comfortable with the basics, you can gradually add complexity and sophistication to your projects, bringing your robotic creations to life in imaginative and innovative ways.

CREATING GUI (GRAPHICAL USER INTERFACE) APPLICATIONS

Overview of GUI Development Options for Raspberry Pi

Graphical User Interfaces (GUIs) enhance the user experience by providing visual and interactive interfaces for Raspberry Pi applications. Whether you're building a user-friendly application or creating a touch-based control panel, there are several GUI development options available for your Raspberry Pi projects.

1. Tkinter

Description: Tkinter is a standard GUI toolkit for Python that provides a set of tools for creating desktop applications with graphical interfaces.

Pros:

- Built-in with Python (no need to install additional libraries).
- Simple to use for creating basic GUIs.
- Suitable for small to medium-sized applications.

Cons:

- Limited in terms of modern design and advanced features.
- May not provide the same level of customization and flexibility as other frameworks.

2. PyQt / PySide

Description: PyQt and PySide are Python bindings for the Qt application framework, which allows you to create powerful and feature-rich GUI applications.

Pros:

- Offers a wide range of UI elements and features.
- Supports modern and visually appealing designs.
- Suitable for both small and large applications.

Cons:

- Requires additional installation and setup.
- Might have a steeper learning curve compared to simpler GUI libraries.

3. Kivy

Description: Kivy is an open-source Python library designed for creating multi-touch applications, making it great for touchscreens and mobile devices.

Pros:

- Focuses on touch-based interfaces.
- Cross-platform support for Windows, macOS, Linux, Android, and iOS.
- Supports complex and interactive UIs.

Cons:

- Might not be as intuitive for traditional desktop applications.
- Requires additional learning if you're not familiar with Kivy's concepts.

4. wxPython

Description: wxPython is a wrapper for the wxWidgets C++ library, providing native-looking GUI applications with a variety of widgets.

Pros:

- Offers a native look and feel across different platforms.
- Provides a good balance between simplicity and features.
- Suitable for both simple and more advanced applications.

Cons:

- Requires installation and setup.
- May not be as modern-looking as some other options.

5. Web-based Interfaces

Description: Creating a web-based interface allows you to access your Raspberry Pi application using a web browser, making it convenient for remote control.

Pros:

- Accessible from any device with a web browser.
- Suitable for applications that require remote access.
- Web development skills can be reused.

Cons:

- Requires knowledge of web development technologies (HTML, CSS, JavaScript).
- May not provide the same level of performance and

responsiveness as native GUIs.

6. Scratch and ScratchGPIO

Description: Scratch is a visual programming language that simplifies the creation of interactive stories, animations, and games.

Pros:

- Ideal for beginners and educational purposes.

- Visual and user-friendly interface.

- Supports interaction with physical components using ScratchGPIO.

Cons:

- Limited to more simple and educational projects.

- Might not be suitable for professional or complex applications.

When developing GUIs for your Raspberry Pi projects, you have a variety of options to choose from, each with its own strengths and limitations. Your choice should be based on factors such as the complexity of your application, your familiarity with the technology, and the desired user experience. Whichever option you choose, GUI development can greatly enhance the usability and visual appeal of your Raspberry Pi projects.

Using Tkinter for Creating Graphical Interfaces

Tkinter is a popular GUI toolkit that comes bundled with Python. It provides a simple way to create graphical interfaces for your Raspberry Pi applications. Whether you're building a basic user interface or a small utility program, Tkinter offers an intuitive approach to designing and interacting with GUIs.

Getting Started with Tkinter:

1. **Import the Tkinter Library**:

```
import tkinter as tk
```

2. **Create a Main Window**:

```
root = tk.Tk()  # Create the main window
root.title("My GUI")  # Set the window title
```

3. **Add Widgets (UI Elements)**: You can add various widgets such as labels, buttons, entry fields, and more.

```
label = tk.Label(root, text="Hello, Tkinter!")  # Create a label
widget
button = tk.Button(root, text="Click Me")  # Create a button
widget
```

4. **Position Widgets using Layout Managers**: Tkinter provides layout managers like **pack, grid**, and **place** to position widgets within the window.

```
label.pack()  # Position label using pack layout manager
button.pack()  # Position button using pack layout manager
```

5. **Start the GUI Main Loop**: The main loop is responsible for handling events and keeping the GUI responsive.

```
root.mainloop()  # Start the GUI main loop
```

Example: Creating a Simple Calculator GUI:

Let's create a basic calculator GUI using Tkinter to perform addition.

```
import tkinter as tk

def add_numbers():
    num1 = float(entry_num1.get())
    num2 = float(entry_num2.get())
    result.set(num1 + num2)

root = tk.Tk()
root.title("Simple Calculator")

entry_num1 = tk.Entry(root)
entry_num2 = tk.Entry(root)
button_add = tk.Button(root, text="Add",
command=add_numbers)
result = tk.StringVar()
label_result = tk.Label(root, textvariable=result)

entry_num1.pack()
entry_num2.pack()
button_add.pack()
label_result.pack()

root.mainloop()
```

In this example, the user enters two numbers in the entry fields, clicks the "Add" button, and the result is displayed using a label.

Pros of Using Tkinter:

- **Simplicity**: Tkinter is easy to learn and use, making it great for beginners.

- **Bundled with Python**: No need to install external libraries; Tkinter is included with Python.

- **Basic Widgets**: Provides common UI elements like buttons, labels, entry fields, and more.

Cons of Using Tkinter:

- **Limited Modernization**: While Tkinter is functional, it might lack the modern look and advanced features of other libraries.

- **Customization Challenges**: Advanced customizations may require more effort and code compared to some other GUI libraries.

Tkinter is a versatile choice for creating graphical interfaces on your Raspberry Pi. It's particularly well-suited for simple applications and educational purposes. By understanding the basics of Tkinter and exploring its capabilities, you can create user-friendly and interactive interfaces for your Raspberry Pi projects.

Designing Interactive Applications

Designing interactive applications is all about creating user experiences that engage, guide, and satisfy users. Whether you're building a game, a utility tool, or a control interface for your Raspberry Pi projects, effective interaction design is crucial for making your applications enjoyable and user-friendly.

1. Understand Your Users:

- **User Persona**: Define your target audience – their needs, goals, preferences, and technical expertise.
- **User Scenarios**: Imagine how users will interact with your application in real-world situations.
- **User Testing**: Gather feedback from users during development to identify pain points and areas for improvement.

2. Prioritize User-Friendly Interfaces:

- **Simplicity**: Keep your interface clean and uncluttered, focusing on the essential features.
- **Consistency**: Use consistent layouts, colors, and fonts to create a cohesive experience.
- **Hierarchy**: Emphasize important elements and content through visual hierarchy and clear contrasts.

3. Navigation and Flow:

- **Intuitive Navigation**: Create a logical flow that guides users through the application without confusion.
- **Clear Signposts**: Use labels, buttons, and icons that clearly indicate the purpose of each element.
- **Feedback**: Provide visual or auditory feedback for user actions, like button presses or form submissions.

4. Interactivity and Engagement:

- **Microinteractions**: Add subtle animations, transitions, and visual effects to enhance the interactive experience.
- **Gamification**: Incorporate game-like elements, such as rewards, challenges, and achievements, to motivate users.

- **Personalization**: Allow users to customize settings or profiles to create a more personalized experience.

5. Responsiveness:

- **Adaptability**: Design applications that work seamlessly across different devices and screen sizes.
- **Touch-Friendly**: If targeting touchscreens, ensure that buttons and controls are large enough and spaced adequately.

6. Accessibility:

- **Inclusive Design**: Consider users with disabilities by ensuring your application is accessible through keyboard navigation, screen readers, and other assistive technologies.
- **Contrast and Text Size**: Use readable fonts, appropriate text sizes, and high contrast for legibility.

7. Error Handling:

- **User-Friendly Errors**: Provide clear and informative error messages that help users understand the problem and provide solutions.
- **Prevention**: Anticipate user errors and design interfaces that minimize the likelihood of mistakes.

8. Testing and Iteration:

- **Usability Testing**: Regularly test your application with real users to identify usability issues and gather feedback.
- **Iterative Design**: Continuously refine and improve your application based on user feedback and observations.

9. Documentation and Help:

- **User Guides**: Provide clear and concise documentation or tooltips that guide users through complex tasks.

- **Contextual Help**: Include contextual help within the application to assist users when needed.

10. Aesthetics and Branding:

- **Visual Identity**: Align your application's design with your brand's visual identity, using consistent colors, logos, and imagery.

- **Aesthetics**: Incorporate a visually pleasing design that resonates with your target audience.

Designing interactive applications for your Raspberry Pi projects involves a delicate balance between functionality, aesthetics, and user-centered design principles. By understanding your users, prioritizing usability, providing engaging interactivity, and continuously refining your design based on feedback, you can create applications that not only fulfill their intended purpose but also delight and engage your audience.

Incorporating Buttons, Input Fields, and Other Widgets

Buttons, input fields, and other widgets are the building blocks of interactive user interfaces. They allow users to provide input, trigger actions, and navigate through your applications. Incorporating these widgets effectively is crucial for creating user-friendly and engaging experiences in your Raspberry Pi projects.

1. Buttons:

Buttons are fundamental for enabling user interactions and

initiating actions. They can be used for tasks like submitting forms, triggering processes, or navigating between screens.

Example Code:

```python
import tkinter as tk

def on_button_click():
    label.config(text="Button Clicked!")

root = tk.Tk()

button = tk.Button(root, text="Click Me",
command=on_button_click)
label = tk.Label(root, text="")

button.pack()
label.pack()

root.mainloop()
```

2. Input Fields:

Input fields allow users to enter text or numeric data. They're essential for collecting user input, such as usernames, passwords, or search queries.

Example Code:

```python
import tkinter as tk

def on_submit():
    entered_text = entry.get()
    label.config(text=f"You entered: {entered_text}")

root = tk.Tk()
```

```
entry = tk.Entry(root)
submit_button = tk.Button(root, text="Submit",
command=on_submit)
label = tk.Label(root, text="")

entry.pack()
submit_button.pack()
label.pack()

root.mainloop()
```

3. Checkboxes and Radio Buttons:

Checkboxes allow users to select one or more options from a list. Radio buttons allow users to choose a single option from a group of choices.

Example Code:

```
import tkinter as tk

def show_selected():
    selected_options = [var1.get(), var2.get(), var3.get()]
    label.config(text=f"Selected options: {',
'.join(selected_options)}")

root = tk.Tk()

var1 = tk.BooleanVar()
var2 = tk.BooleanVar()
var3 = tk.BooleanVar()

check1 = tk.Checkbutton(root, text="Option 1", variable=var1)
check2 = tk.Checkbutton(root, text="Option 2", variable=var2)
check3 = tk.Checkbutton(root, text="Option 3", variable=var3)
submit_button = tk.Button(root, text="Show Selected",
command=show_selected)
label = tk.Label(root, text="")
```

```
check1.pack()
check2.pack()
check3.pack()
submit_button.pack()
label.pack()

root.mainloop()
```

4. Dropdown Menus:

Dropdown menus provide users with a list of options that can be selected from a drop-down list.

Example Code:

```
import tkinter as tk
from tkinter import ttk

def on_selection(event):
    selected_item = combo.get()
    label.config(text=f"Selected: {selected_item}")

root = tk.Tk()

options = ["Option 1", "Option 2", "Option 3"]
combo = ttk.Combobox(root, values=options)
combo.bind("<<ComboboxSelected>>", on_selection)
label = tk.Label(root, text="")

combo.pack()
label.pack()

root.mainloop()
```

Incorporating buttons, input fields, checkboxes, radio buttons, dropdown menus, and other widgets into your GUI applications empowers users to interact with your projects in meaningful ways. By understanding the purpose of each widget and its associated event handling, you can create intuitive and user-friendly interfaces that make your Raspberry Pi projects more engaging and accessible.

Developing a Weather App with a Graphical Interface

Creating a weather app with a graphical interface allows users to easily access and visualize weather information. With Python and libraries like Tkinter and requests, you can build a simple yet effective weather app that fetches weather data from an API and presents it to users in an intuitive way. Here's a step-by-step guide to developing a weather app:

1. Set Up Your Development Environment:

Make sure you have Python installed on your Raspberry Pi. You'll also need the **requests** library to make API requests. You can install it using:

```
pip install requests
```

2. Choose a Weather API:

There are several weather APIs available that provide weather data in JSON format. OpenWeatherMap, WeatherAPI, and Weatherstack are popular options. Sign up for an API key on your chosen platform.

3. Design the GUI:

Use Tkinter to design the graphical interface of your weather app. Create labels, entry fields, and buttons for user interaction. For example:

```
import tkinter as tk

def get_weather():
    # Fetch weather data from the API and update the interface
    pass

root = tk.Tk()
root.title("Weather App")

city_label = tk.Label(root, text="Enter City:")
city_entry = tk.Entry(root)
get_button = tk.Button(root, text="Get Weather",
command=get_weather)
weather_label = tk.Label(root, text="Weather: ")
temperature_label = tk.Label(root, text="Temperature: ")

city_label.pack()
city_entry.pack()
get_button.pack()
weather_label.pack()
temperature_label.pack()

root.mainloop()
```

4. Fetch Weather Data from the API:

Use the **requests** library to make an API request and retrieve weather data based on the city entered by the user. Parse the JSON response and extract relevant information.

```
import requests

def get_weather():
    city = city_entry.get()
    api_key = "YOUR_API_KEY"
```

```
    url =
f"https://api.openweathermap.org/data/2.5/weather?q={city}&a
ppid={api_key}&units=metric"

    response = requests.get(url)
    weather_data = response.json()

    weather_label.config(text=f"Weather:
{weather_data['weather'][0]['description']}")
    temperature_label.config(text=f"Temperature:
{weather_data['main']['temp']}°C")
```

5. Run the App:

Run your weather app, enter a city name, and click the "Get Weather" button. The app should fetch and display weather information for the specified city.

6. Enhancements:

- Add error handling for cases when the API request fails or the city name is invalid.
- Include additional weather data such as humidity, wind speed, and more.
- Improve the app's visual design by using more widgets, fonts, and colors.
- Consider adding icons to represent weather conditions.

Developing a weather app with a graphical interface is a great way to practice using APIs, working with JSON data, and designing user-friendly applications. By following these steps and customizing the app to your needs, you can create a functional weather app that provides users with up-to-date weather information at their fingertips on your Raspberry Pi.

WORKING WITH CAMERAS

Setting Up and Configuring the Raspberry Pi Camera Module

The Raspberry Pi Camera Module is a versatile accessory that allows you to capture photos and videos directly from your Raspberry Pi. Whether you're interested in photography, video streaming, surveillance, or robotics, the Camera Module offers a wide range of possibilities. Here's a guide to setting up and configuring the Raspberry Pi Camera Module:

1. **Hardware Requirements**:

- Raspberry Pi (any model with a CSI camera port)
- Raspberry Pi Camera Module (Standard or NoIR, depending on your needs)
- Camera cable (included with the Camera Module)

2. **Physical Installation**:

- Make sure your Raspberry Pi is powered off and unplugged.
- Insert the camera cable into the CSI camera port on the

Raspberry Pi.

- Open the camera port by gently lifting the plastic tabs on either side of the port.
- Insert the cable, ensuring the blue side faces the Ethernet port.

3. **Enabling the Camera Interface**:

- Boot up your Raspberry Pi.
- Open the terminal or SSH into your Pi.
- Run the following command to open the Raspberry Pi Configuration tool:

```
sudo raspi-config
```

- Navigate to "Interfacing Options" and select "Camera."
- Choose "Yes" to enable the camera interface.
- Reboot your Raspberry Pi for the changes to take effect.

4. **Testing the Camera**:

- After enabling the camera interface, reboot your Raspberry Pi.
- Open the terminal and enter the following command to capture an image:

```
raspistill -o test_image.jpg
```

- The captured image will be saved as "test_image.jpg" in the current directory.

5. **Basic Configuration Options**:

- The **raspistill** and **raspivid** commands allow you to capture images and videos, respectively. Use the **--help** flag to see all available options.
- You can adjust parameters such as exposure, white balance, resolution, and more to customize the quality and characteristics of your media.

6. **Advanced Configuration**:

- For more advanced configurations, you can modify the **/boot/config.txt** file to adjust camera settings like exposure, contrast, saturation, and more.
- The official Raspberry Pi documentation provides a comprehensive list of configuration options for the camera module.

7. **Streaming and Projects**:

- The Camera Module is not limited to capturing images and videos; you can use it for live video streaming, time-lapse photography, motion detection, and more.
- Numerous libraries and software packages are available for integrating the Camera Module into your projects.

8. **Camera Accessories**:

- To protect the camera and improve image quality, consider using camera cases, lenses, filters, and infrared lighting (for NoIR models).

The Raspberry Pi Camera Module offers a convenient and flexible way to capture images and videos directly from your Raspberry Pi. By following these steps to set up and configure the camera, you can start exploring various photography, video, and streaming projects to enhance your Raspberry Pi experience.

Capturing Photos and Videos with Python

The Raspberry Pi Camera Module enables you to capture photos and videos programmatically using Python. This functionality is useful for creating time-lapse videos, monitoring applications, robotics projects, and more.

1. Capturing Photos with Python:

You can use the **picamera** library to capture photos easily.

```
from picamera import PiCamera
import time

camera = PiCamera()

# Capture a photo
camera.capture("photo.jpg")

camera.close()
```

In this example, a photo is captured and saved as "photo.jpg". You can customize various camera settings using methods like **resolution, rotation, exposure_mode**, etc.

2. Capturing Videos with Python:

To capture videos, you can use the **picamera** library as well.

```
from picamera import PiCamera
import time
```

```
camera = PiCamera()

# Capture a 10-second video
camera.start_recording("video.h264")
time.sleep(10)
camera.stop_recording()

camera.close()
```

This example captures a 10-second video and saves it as "video.h264". You can adjust video settings such as **resolution, framerate**, and more.

3. Adding Annotations:

You can overlay text and other annotations on your photos and videos.

```
from picamera import PiCamera
import time

camera = PiCamera()

camera.annotate_text = "Hello, Raspberry Pi!"

# Capture a photo with annotation
camera.capture("annotated_photo.jpg")

camera.close()
```

4. Continuous Capture:

You can capture multiple photos or record continuous videos.

```
from picamera import PiCamera
import time
```

```
camera = PiCamera()

# Capture multiple photos
for i in range(5):
    camera.capture(f"photo_{i}.jpg")
    time.sleep(2)  # Wait for 2 seconds between captures

camera.close()
```

5. Advanced Features:

- The **picamera** library provides advanced features like capturing time-lapse sequences, recording with motion detection, and more.

- You can use the **subprocess** module to convert captured H.264 videos to other formats (e.g., MP4).

6. Streaming Video:

Streaming video from the camera to a display or over a network is possible using libraries like **picamera** and **cv2** (OpenCV).

Capturing photos and videos with Python and the Raspberry Pi Camera Module opens up a world of creative possibilities. Whether you're building a surveillance system, documenting a project's progress, or experimenting with photography, the Camera Module and the **picamera** library provide the tools you need to integrate multimedia functionality into your Raspberry Pi projects.

Image Processing and Manipulation Using Python Libraries

Image processing and manipulation play a vital role in a wide range of applications, from enhancing photographs to analyzing medical images and creating digital art. Python offers powerful libraries that allow you to perform various image-related tasks with ease.

1. Pillow (PIL Fork):

Pillow is a user-friendly library for opening, manipulating, and saving various image file formats. It's often used for basic image operations and simple transformations.

Example: Opening and Saving Images:

```
from PIL import Image

# Open an image
image = Image.open("image.jpg")

# Display image properties
print(image.format, image.size, image.mode)

# Save image in different format
image.save("new_image.png")
```

2. OpenCV:

OpenCV is a versatile computer vision library that provides advanced image processing, computer vision algorithms, and machine learning capabilities.

Example: Image Filtering and Edges Detection:

```
import cv2

# Read an image
image = cv2.imread("image.jpg")
```

```
# Convert to grayscale
gray_image = cv2.cvtColor(image, cv2.COLOR_BGR2GRAY)

# Apply Gaussian blur
blurred_image = cv2.GaussianBlur(gray_image, (5, 5), 0)

# Detect edges using Canny
edges = cv2.Canny(blurred_image, threshold1=30,
threshold2=70)

# Display and save the result
cv2.imshow("Edges", edges)
cv2.imwrite("edges.jpg", edges)
cv2.waitKey(0)
cv2.destroyAllWindows()
```

3. scikit-image:

scikit-image is a library specifically designed for image processing. It offers various functions for tasks like segmentation, feature extraction, and color manipulation.

Example: Image Thresholding:

```
from skimage import io, color, filters
import matplotlib.pyplot as plt

# Load an image
image = io.imread("image.jpg")

# Convert to grayscale
gray_image = color.rgb2gray(image)

# Apply thresholding
threshold = filters.threshold_otsu(gray_image)
binary_image = gray_image > threshold
```

```
# Display the original and binary images
fig, axes = plt.subplots(1, 2, figsize=(8, 4))
ax = axes.ravel()
ax[0].imshow(gray_image, cmap=plt.cm.gray)
ax[0].set_title("Original Image")
ax[1].imshow(binary_image, cmap=plt.cm.gray)
ax[1].set_title("Binary Image")
plt.show()
```

4. numpy:

While not solely an image processing library, numpy is a fundamental package for scientific computing in Python. It's often used for performing basic mathematical and array operations on images.

Example: Image Histogram Equalization:

```
import cv2
import numpy as np
import matplotlib.pyplot as plt

# Read an image
image = cv2.imread("image.jpg", cv2.IMREAD_GRAYSCALE)

# Apply histogram equalization
equalized_image = cv2.equalizeHist(image)

# Display original and equalized images
plt.figure(figsize=(10, 5))
plt.subplot(121)
plt.imshow(image, cmap="gray")
plt.title("Original Image")
plt.subplot(122)
plt.imshow(equalized_image, cmap="gray")
plt.title("Equalized Image")
plt.show()
```

Python's versatile image processing libraries offer a wide array of tools for tasks ranging from basic operations like opening and saving images to more advanced tasks like edge detection, filtering, and segmentation. Whether you're a hobbyist, a researcher, or a professional, these libraries empower you to explore, analyze, and manipulate images for various applications.

Building a Basic Surveillance System

Creating a basic surveillance system using a Raspberry Pi and a camera module is a practical and cost-effective way to monitor an area. Whether you want to keep an eye on your home, office, or any other location, this project can help you achieve that. Here's a step-by-step guide to building a basic surveillance system:

1. Gather the Required Hardware:

- Raspberry Pi (any model with a camera port)
- Raspberry Pi Camera Module (Standard or NoIR, depending on your needs)
- Camera cable
- MicroSD card (with Raspbian or Raspberry Pi OS installed)
- Power supply for the Raspberry Pi
- Ethernet or Wi-Fi connection for remote access

2. Set Up the Raspberry Pi:

- Insert the microSD card with the operating system into the Raspberry Pi.
- Connect the Raspberry Pi to a monitor, keyboard, and mouse for initial setup.

- Follow the setup instructions to configure the Wi-Fi, set passwords, and enable SSH for remote access.

3. Connect and Enable the Camera Module:

- Insert the camera cable into the CSI camera port on the Raspberry Pi.
- Open the terminal and run **sudo raspi-config**.
- Navigate to "Interfacing Options" and select "Camera."
- Choose "Yes" to enable the camera interface.
- Reboot the Raspberry Pi for the changes to take effect.

4. Install Required Software:

- Update the package list and install the **motion** package (a motion detection software) using **sudo apt-get update && sudo apt-get install motion**.

5. Configure the Surveillance Software:

- Edit the configuration file using **sudo nano /etc/motion/motion.conf**.
- Adjust settings such as resolution, framerate, target directory, and more.
- Save the changes and exit the text editor.

6. Start the Surveillance System:

- Start the motion service using **sudo service motion start**.
- Access the web interface by entering the Raspberry Pi's IP address and port 8081 in a web browser (e.g., **http://raspberry_pi_ip:8081**).
- You can adjust settings and view live streams and captured images/videos through the web interface.

7. Optional Enhancements:

- Use the **motion** software's features to set up motion detection zones, email alerts, and custom triggers.
- Consider automating the system to start on boot using **sudo systemctl enable motion**.

8. Remote Access and Monitoring:

- Ensure your Raspberry Pi is accessible via Wi-Fi or Ethernet.
- Access the surveillance system remotely using the web interface from any device connected to the same network.

9. Storage and Retention:

- Regularly clean or back up the storage directory to avoid running out of space.
- Consider using external storage solutions or cloud storage to retain recordings.

10. Security Considerations:

- Ensure that your Raspberry Pi and surveillance system are secured with strong passwords and firewall settings.

Building a basic surveillance system using a Raspberry Pi and a camera module is a straightforward project that offers a valuable solution for monitoring areas of interest. While this project provides a simple setup, you can further enhance and customize the system to meet your specific needs, making it an effective tool for home security, monitoring pets, observing wildlife, and more.

NETWORKING AND IOT (INTERNET OF THINGS)

Connecting Raspberry Pi to Wi-Fi Networks

Connecting your Raspberry Pi to Wi-Fi networks is essential for accessing the internet, updating software, and enabling remote communication. Whether you're using a Raspberry Pi for home projects, development, or IoT applications, setting up Wi-Fi connectivity is straightforward. Here's a step-by-step guide to help you connect your Raspberry Pi to Wi-Fi networks:

1. Gather What You Need:

- Raspberry Pi (any model with Wi-Fi capability)
- MicroSD card (with Raspbian or Raspberry Pi OS installed)
- Power supply for the Raspberry Pi
- Wi-Fi network name (SSID) and password

2. Boot Up Your Raspberry Pi:

- Insert the microSD card with the operating system into the Raspberry Pi.

- Connect the Raspberry Pi to a monitor, keyboard, and mouse for initial setup.

3. Configure Wi-Fi Using the Desktop Environment:

- If you're using the Raspberry Pi with a graphical desktop environment:
  - Click on the Wi-Fi icon in the top-right corner of the screen.
  - Select your Wi-Fi network from the list.
  - Enter the Wi-Fi password when prompted.
  - Your Raspberry Pi will automatically connect to the selected network.

4. Configure Wi-Fi Using the Command Line:

- Open a terminal window (command line).
- Edit the **wpa_supplicant.conf** file by running the command: **sudo nano /etc/wpa_supplicant/wpa_supplicant.conf**
- Add the following lines, replacing **"Your_SSID"** and **"Your_Password"** with your actual Wi-Fi network name and password:

```
network={
    ssid="Your_SSID"
    psk="Your_Password"
}
```

- Save the file by pressing **Ctrl + O**, and exit the text editor by pressing **Ctrl + X**.

5. Reboot the Raspberry Pi:

- Restart your Raspberry Pi to apply the Wi-Fi settings: **sudo** reboot

6. Verify the Wi-Fi Connection:

- After the reboot, check if your Raspberry Pi is connected to Wi-Fi:

  - If you're using the command line, you can run **ifconfig** to see network information.

  - If you're using the desktop environment, the Wi-Fi icon should indicate a successful connection.

7. Troubleshooting:

- If you encounter connection issues, ensure that the Wi-Fi network name and password are entered correctly.

- Check if the Wi-Fi network is available and functioning.

- Make sure that you're using the correct country code in the **wpa_supplicant.conf** file (if required).

8. Additional Considerations:

- You can configure Wi-Fi settings for multiple networks by adding multiple **network** sections in the **wpa_supplicant.conf** file.

- If you're using headless mode (without a monitor), you can create the **wpa_supplicant.conf** file on the microSD card before booting the Raspberry Pi.

Connecting your Raspberry Pi to Wi-Fi networks allows you to access online resources, update software, and enable remote communication. Whether you prefer using the graphical interface or the command line, setting up Wi-Fi is a crucial step in maximizing the capabilities of your Raspberry Pi for various projects and applications.

Sending and Receiving Data Over the Internet

Sending and receiving data over the internet is a fundamental capability that opens the door to a wide range of applications, from remote monitoring and control to real-time data exchange. Whether you're building IoT projects, web applications, or communication systems, understanding how to transmit and receive data is essential. Here's a guide to help you get started with sending and receiving data over the internet using Python:

1. Data Transmission Basics:

Data transmission involves sending information from one device to another over a network, typically using protocols like HTTP, MQTT, TCP/IP, or WebSocket. Data can be in various formats, including text, JSON, XML, images, or binary data.

2. Sending Data with Python:

To send data over the internet using Python, you'll often use libraries like **requests** for HTTP communication, or **paho-mqtt** for MQTT communication.

Example: Sending an HTTP POST Request:

```
import requests

data = {"key": "value"}
response = requests.post("https://example.com/api", json=data)

print(response.status_code)
```

```
print(response.text)
```

3. Receiving Data with Python:

Receiving data involves setting up a server or client to listen for incoming data. Libraries like **flask** and **socket** facilitate this process.

Example: Creating a Basic Web Server with Flask:

```python
from flask import Flask

app = Flask(__name__)

@app.route("/")
def hello():
    return "Hello, world!"

if __name__ == "__main__":
    app.run(host="0.0.0.0", port=80)
```

Example: Creating a Basic TCP Server with Socket:

```python
import socket

server = socket.socket(socket.AF_INET, socket.SOCK_STREAM)
server.bind(("0.0.0.0", 12345))
server.listen()

while True:
    client, address = server.accept()
    data = client.recv(1024)
    print(f"Received: {data.decode()}")
    client.close()
```

4. Security and Authentication:

When sending and receiving data over the internet, security is crucial. Use protocols that support encryption (e.g., HTTPS, MQTT over TLS), implement authentication mechanisms (e.g., API keys, OAuth), and validate data inputs to prevent vulnerabilities.

5. Error Handling and Resilience:

Network connections can be unreliable. Implement error handling, timeouts, and retries to ensure your application gracefully handles communication failures.

6. Scalability and Performance:

For applications that require handling large amounts of data or high traffic, consider optimizing performance by using asynchronous programming, load balancing, and caching.

7. Cloud Services and APIs:

Leverage cloud services and APIs to simplify data transmission and storage. Services like AWS, Azure, and Google Cloud offer powerful tools for building and scaling applications.

8. Real-Time Communication:

For real-time data exchange, consider using protocols like WebSocket, which enables full-duplex communication between clients and servers.

9. Data Formats:

Choose appropriate data formats based on the nature of your application. JSON is widely used for structured data, while binary formats like Protocol Buffers can be more efficient for large datasets.

Sending and receiving data over the internet is a fundamental skill for modern development. Whether you're building web applications,

IoT devices, or communication systems, understanding the principles of data transmission, security, and network protocols will empower you to create robust and efficient applications that can exchange information with other devices and services across the internet.

Introduction to MQTT for IoT Communication

MQTT (Message Queuing Telemetry Transport) is a lightweight and efficient messaging protocol designed for communication between devices in Internet of Things (IoT) and remote sensing applications. MQTT provides a reliable and low-overhead way to exchange data between devices, making it a popular choice for IoT scenarios where bandwidth and power efficiency are essential.

1. Publish-Subscribe Model:

At the heart of MQTT is the publish-subscribe model. In this model, devices can be categorized into publishers and subscribers. Publishers send messages (also known as "publishing" messages) to specific topics. Subscribers receive messages by subscribing to topics of interest. This decoupled approach allows devices to communicate without direct knowledge of each other.

2. Topics:

Topics are hierarchical strings used to categorize messages. Subscribers can choose to subscribe to specific topics, allowing them to receive only the messages relevant to their interests. For example, a weather station could publish temperature data to the topic "weather/temperature."

3. Quality of Service (QoS):

MQTT supports different levels of Quality of Service:

- QoS 0: The message is delivered once without acknowledgment. This level has the least reliability.
- QoS 1: The message is guaranteed to be delivered at least once, but duplicates may occur.
- QoS 2: The message is guaranteed to be delivered exactly once by using a four-step handshake.

Higher QoS levels offer increased reliability but involve more network overhead.

4. Retained Messages:

Retained messages are messages that are stored by the MQTT broker and sent to new subscribers when they connect to a topic. This is useful for providing the latest information to new subscribers without the need for immediate publishing.

5. Last Will and Testament (LWT):

Devices can set a "last will" message that will be published by the broker if the device disconnects unexpectedly. This feature is particularly useful for indicating device status changes or errors.

6. MQTT Broker:

An MQTT broker is a central server that acts as an intermediary between publishers and subscribers. It receives messages from publishers and routes them to the appropriate subscribers based on topic subscriptions. Popular MQTT brokers include Mosquitto, HiveMQ, and EMQ.

7. Use Cases for MQTT:

- IoT Sensor Networks: MQTT is well-suited for transmitting

data from sensors to a central hub or cloud service.

- Home Automation: Smart home devices can communicate with each other using MQTT to control lights, thermostats, and more.

- Industrial Automation: MQTT's low overhead makes it suitable for real-time monitoring and control in industrial environments.

- Telemetry: Vehicles, airplanes, and machinery can use MQTT to send telemetry data for analysis and monitoring.

8. MQTT Libraries and Implementations:

There are MQTT client libraries available for various programming languages, making it easy to integrate MQTT communication into your projects. Some popular MQTT libraries include Paho for Python, Eclipse Paho for Java, and MQTT.js for JavaScript.

MQTT is a powerful and efficient protocol for IoT communication, offering a publish-subscribe model that allows devices to exchange data with minimal overhead. Its support for various QoS levels, retained messages, and other features makes it a versatile choice for a wide range of IoT applications. By understanding MQTT's principles, you can leverage it to build reliable and scalable IoT systems that efficiently exchange data among devices.

Building a Home Automation System

A home automation system allows you to control various aspects of your home, such as lighting, appliances, security, and entertainment, using technology. With the rise of IoT devices and smart technologies, building a home automation system has become more accessible than ever. Here's a comprehensive guide to help you create your own home automation system:

1. Define Your Goals:

Determine the aspects of your home you want to automate. Common areas include lighting, HVAC (heating, ventilation, air conditioning), security cameras, door locks, entertainment systems, and more.

2. Choose a Platform:

Select a home automation platform or hub that will serve as the central control unit for your devices. Popular options include:

- **Smart Speakers**: Devices like Amazon Echo, Google Home, or Apple HomePod can serve as a hub for voice-controlled automation.
- **Smart Hubs**: Dedicated hubs like Samsung SmartThings, Hubitat, or Home Assistant provide more control over various devices and protocols.

3. Select Devices and Components:

Choose IoT devices and components compatible with your chosen platform. Consider devices like smart plugs, smart bulbs, smart thermostats, smart locks, motion sensors, and security cameras.

4. Set Up Communication Protocols:

Different devices might use various communication protocols, such as Wi-Fi, Zigbee, Z-Wave, or Bluetooth. Ensure that your chosen platform supports the protocols of your selected devices.

5. Integration and Automation:

Use your chosen platform to create automation routines or scenes. These routines allow you to specify triggers (events that initiate actions) and actions (what happens when a trigger occurs). For example:

- "Good Morning" Routine: Turn on lights, adjust thermostat, and play news briefing when you say "Good morning" to your smart speaker.
- "Home Security" Scene: Lock doors, arm security cameras, and turn off lights when you leave home.

6. Voice Control:

If your platform supports it, integrate voice control. With voice commands, you can control devices and trigger routines using smart speakers like Amazon Echo or Google Home.

7. Remote Control:

Many platforms offer mobile apps that enable you to control and monitor your home automation system remotely. This is especially useful for checking security cameras or adjusting settings while you're away.

8. Security and Privacy:

Ensure that your home automation system follows security best practices. Set strong passwords, enable two-factor authentication, and regularly update device firmware to prevent vulnerabilities.

9. Expand and Customize:

As you become more comfortable with your home automation system, you can expand by adding new devices, integrating third-party services, and customizing automation based on your preferences.

10. Consider Energy Efficiency:

Home automation can lead to energy savings. For example, smart thermostats can learn your habits and adjust the temperature accordingly, saving energy when you're not at home.

11. Experiment and Learn:

Building a home automation system is an ongoing process. Experiment with different devices, automation routines, and configurations to find what works best for your lifestyle and needs.

12. Balance Automation and Manual Control:

While automation can make life more convenient, remember to strike a balance. Certain tasks might still be best controlled manually, especially if unexpected situations arise.

Building a home automation system lets you harness the power of IoT devices and smart technologies to create a more comfortable and efficient living space. By defining your goals, selecting compatible devices, setting up automation routines, and prioritizing security, you can transform your home into a smart, connected environment that enhances your quality of life.

Creating a Web-Based Dashboard for IoT Control

A web-based dashboard offers a user-friendly interface to control and monitor your IoT devices from anywhere with an internet connection. It provides a central hub for managing different aspects of your IoT system, such as turning devices on/off, adjusting settings, and viewing real-time data. Here's a step-by-step guide to creating a web-based dashboard for IoT control:

1. Choose a Development Approach:

There are several ways to create a web-based dashboard. You can use HTML, CSS, and JavaScript to build a frontend from scratch, or you can use frameworks like React, Vue.js, or Angular for a more structured approach. For backend development, you can use languages like Python, Node.js, or Ruby.

2. Define Dashboard Features:

Determine the features you want to include in your dashboard. These could include device control buttons, real-time data visualization, status indicators, and user authentication.

3. Set Up a Web Server:

You'll need a web server to host your dashboard. This server will handle user requests, serve HTML and other assets, and interact with your IoT devices. You can use popular web server technologies like Apache, Nginx, or Node.js.

4. Establish Communication with IoT Devices:

Your dashboard needs a way to communicate with your IoT devices. Depending on the devices and protocols you're using, this could involve HTTP requests, MQTT, WebSocket, or other communication methods.

5. Create the Frontend:

Design the user interface of your dashboard using HTML, CSS, and JavaScript (or a frontend framework). Consider using responsive design principles to ensure the dashboard works well on different devices and screen sizes.

6. Implement User Authentication:

If your dashboard will be accessed by multiple users, implement user authentication to secure access. Common authentication methods include username/password login, OAuth, and JWT (JSON Web Tokens).

7. Display Real-Time Data:

If your IoT devices provide real-time data (such as sensor readings), integrate data visualization libraries like Chart.js or D3.js to display graphs and charts that update dynamically.

8. Implement Device Control:

Create buttons, sliders, or switches in your dashboard to control IoT devices. When users interact with these controls, your dashboard should send commands to the devices through the established communication channel.

9. Test and Debug:

Thoroughly test your dashboard to ensure that all features work as expected. Pay attention to responsiveness, data accuracy, and user experience. Debug any issues that arise during testing.

10. Deploy and Host:

Choose a hosting solution for your dashboard. You can use cloud services like AWS, Heroku, or Firebase, or you can host it on your own server. Ensure that your chosen hosting environment supports the technologies you're using.

11. Monitor and Maintain:

Regularly monitor your dashboard's performance and responsiveness. Keep your software and libraries updated to ensure security and compatibility.

12. Continuous Improvement:

Collect feedback from users and continuously improve your dashboard based on their needs. Consider adding new features, enhancing the user interface, and optimizing performance.

Creating a web-based dashboard for IoT control empowers you to efficiently manage and monitor your connected devices from anywhere. By following these steps and selecting the appropriate technologies, you can build a user-friendly and functional dashboard that enhances your IoT experience and simplifies device management.

DATA STORAGE AND DATABASE INTEGRATION

Storing Data Locally on Raspberry Pi

Storing data locally on a Raspberry Pi is a common requirement for various projects, from logging sensor data to creating databases for applications. Whether you need to store text files, images, databases, or other types of data, the Raspberry Pi provides built-in storage options that you can leverage. Here's a guide on how to store data locally on a Raspberry Pi:

1. Choose the Storage Medium:

Raspberry Pi models typically use microSD cards as the primary storage medium. However, some models also support USB drives or external hard drives for additional storage capacity. Choose the storage medium that suits your project's needs.

2. Mounting External Storage (if applicable):

If you're using external storage like a USB drive or an external hard drive, you might need to manually mount it to make it accessible. The Raspberry Pi's operating system should automatically detect and mount USB drives, but if not, you can use commands like **lsblk** and **mount** to manage storage devices.

3. Creating Directories:

Before storing data, create directories (folders) to organize your data. You can use the command line or a file manager to create directories. For example, to create a directory named "data," use the command: **mkdir data**

4. Storing Text Data:

To store text data, you can use text editors like **nano** or **vim** to create and edit text files. For example, to create a text file named "notes.txt" and add some content, use the command: **nano notes.txt**

5. Storing Binary Data:

For binary data like images, videos, or executables, you can simply copy or move the files to the desired directory. For example, to copy a file named "image.jpg" to the "data" directory, use the command: **cp image.jpg data/**

6. Using Databases:

For structured data storage, you can set up databases like SQLite or MySQL. These databases allow you to create tables, insert data, and perform queries.

Example: Using SQLite:

```
# Install SQLite
sudo apt-get install sqlite3

# Create a new SQLite database file
sqlite3 mydatabase.db
```

```
# Inside the SQLite shell
sqlite> CREATE TABLE users (id INTEGER PRIMARY KEY, username
TEXT, email TEXT);
sqlite> INSERT INTO users (username, email) VALUES ('john',
'john@example.com');
sqlite> .exit
```

7. Backing Up Data:

Regularly back up your data to prevent data loss. You can create backup scripts or use tools like **rsync** to automate this process.

8. Monitoring Storage:

Use commands like **df** to check the available disk space on your storage medium. This helps you avoid running out of space.

9. Security Considerations:

Ensure that your data is protected by setting appropriate file permissions and regularly updating your Raspberry Pi's operating system to patch security vulnerabilities.

10. Using File Compression:

If you need to save space, consider using file compression tools like **zip** or **tar** to compress and archive directories.

11. Ejecting External Storage Safely:

If you're using external storage, make sure to safely eject it before physically disconnecting it from the Raspberry Pi. This helps prevent data corruption.

Storing data locally on a Raspberry Pi is a versatile capability that supports a wide range of projects. Whether you're storing text files, binary data, or structured data in databases, understanding how to manage and organize your data effectively will help you create reliable and efficient applications on your Raspberry Pi.

Working with Files and Directories in Python

Files and directories are fundamental components of any computer system, and Python provides powerful built-in libraries to interact with them. Whether you need to read or write data, manage directories, or perform file operations, Python offers versatile tools to handle these tasks efficiently. Here's a comprehensive guide on working with files and directories in Python:

1. Opening and Reading Files:

You can use the built-in **open()** function to open files for reading or writing. The **read()** method reads the entire content of a file.

```python
# Open and read a text file
with open("myfile.txt", "r") as file:
    content = file.read()
    print(content)
```

2. Writing to Files:

You can open files in write mode using the **"w"** flag. The **write()** method writes data to the file.

```python
# Open and write to a text file
with open("output.txt", "w") as file:
    file.write("Hello, world!")
```

3. Appending to Files:

To add content to an existing file without overwriting its contents, open the file in append mode using the **"a"** flag.

```
# Append to an existing text file
with open("log.txt", "a") as file:
    file.write("New log entry\n")
```

4. Reading Line by Line:

You can read a file line by line using a loop.

```
# Read a file line by line
with open("data.txt", "r") as file:
    for line in file:
        print(line.strip())  # Remove newline characters
```

5. Working with Binary Files:

For binary files like images or videos, open the file in binary mode using the **"rb"** or **"wb"** flags.

6. Managing Directories:

The **os** module provides functions to work with directories, including creating, removing, and listing directories.

```
import os

# Create a new directory
os.mkdir("new_directory")

# Remove a directory
os.rmdir("old_directory")

# List files in a directory
files = os.listdir("my_folder")
print(files)
```

7. Path Operations:

The **pathlib** module offers an object-oriented approach to working with file paths and directories.

```
from pathlib import Path

# Create a Path object
path = Path("my_folder")

# List files in a directory
files = [file.name for file in path.iterdir() if file.is_file()]
print(files)
```

8. Handling Exceptions:

When working with files, exceptions like **FileNotFoundError** and **PermissionError** can occur. Use try-except blocks to handle these exceptions gracefully.

```
try:
    with open("file.txt", "r") as file:
        content = file.read()
except FileNotFoundError:
    print("File not found.")
except PermissionError:
    print("Permission denied.")
```

9. Closing Files:

Although using the **with** statement automatically closes files when done, you can explicitly close files using the **close()** method.

```
file = open("data.txt", "r")
content = file.read()
file.close()
```

10. Context Managers and with Statement:

The **with** statement ensures that files are properly closed after use, even if exceptions occur.

```
with open("data.txt", "r") as file:
    content = file.read()
# File is automatically closed after exiting the block
```

Python's file and directory manipulation capabilities enable you to work seamlessly with various types of data. By understanding how to open, read, write, and manage files and directories, you'll be well-equipped to handle data storage and retrieval tasks effectively in your Python programs.

Introduction to SQLite Databases

SQLite is a lightweight, embedded, open-source relational database management system that is widely used for managing structured data. Unlike traditional database systems, SQLite doesn't require a separate server or setup; it's integrated into the application itself, making it a convenient choice for projects that need local data storage. Here's an introduction to SQLite databases and their key features:

1. Embedded Database:

SQLite is a serverless, self-contained database engine. This means that the database is stored as a single file on the disk and doesn't require a separate server process to manage it. This makes SQLite suitable for applications that need a local database without the overhead of a full-fledged database server.

2. Relational Database:

SQLite is a relational database, which means it organizes data into tables with predefined schemas. Each table consists of rows and columns, where rows represent individual records, and columns represent attributes of those records. Relationships between tables can be established through keys.

3. SQL Support:

SQLite supports SQL (Structured Query Language) for defining, manipulating, and querying data. You can use SQL statements to create tables, insert data, update records, retrieve information, and perform complex queries.

4. Key Features:

- **Zero Configuration**: SQLite doesn't require complex configuration or installation. You can start using it by including its library in your application.
- **Cross-Platform**: SQLite is available on various platforms, including Windows, macOS, Linux, and mobile platforms like Android and iOS.
- **ACID Compliance**: SQLite is ACID-compliant, ensuring data integrity and reliability through Atomicity, Consistency, Isolation, and Durability principles.
- **Transactions**: You can use transactions to group a sequence

of database operations into a single unit. Transactions provide consistency and help maintain data integrity.

- **Indexes**: SQLite supports indexing for faster data retrieval. Indexes are particularly useful for speeding up queries on large datasets.

- **Small Memory Footprint**: SQLite is designed to be memory-efficient, making it suitable for resource-constrained environments.

- **No Separate Server**: As an embedded database, SQLite doesn't require running a separate server process. It operates within the application's address space.

5. Use Cases:

SQLite databases are well-suited for a range of applications:

- Mobile Apps: Many mobile apps use SQLite for storing local data, such as user preferences, cached data, and more.

- Desktop Applications: Desktop software can utilize SQLite to manage local databases for tasks like data storage, logging, and reporting.

- Web Browsers: Some web browsers use SQLite to manage bookmarks, history, and other user-related data.

- IoT Devices: SQLite's lightweight nature makes it a good choice for storing data on resource-constrained IoT devices.

- Prototyping and Development: SQLite databases are ideal for prototyping, testing, and development stages of software projects.

6. Getting Started:

To start using SQLite, you can interact with it using command-line tools or integrate it into your programming language of choice. Python, for example, provides the **sqlite3** module for interacting with SQLite databases.

SQLite databases provide a convenient and efficient way to store structured data within your applications. Their lightweight nature, relational capabilities, and support for SQL make them a powerful choice for a wide range of use cases, from mobile apps and desktop software to IoT devices and more. Whether you're developing a simple application or a complex system, SQLite databases offer reliable local data storage and management capabilities.

Reading and Writing Data to Databases

Reading and writing data to databases is a fundamental aspect of managing structured information. In the context of databases like SQLite, it involves using SQL (Structured Query Language) statements to insert, retrieve, update, and delete data. Here's a comprehensive guide on how to read and write data to databases using Python's **sqlite3** module with SQLite as an example:

1. Connecting to the Database:

To interact with an SQLite database in Python, you need to establish a connection using the **sqlite3.connect()** function.

```
import sqlite3

# Connect to an SQLite database or create a new one
```

```
conn = sqlite3.connect('my_database.db')
```

2. Creating Tables:

Before you can store data, you need to define the structure of your data using tables. Use SQL's **CREATE TABLE** statement to create tables with columns and their respective data types.

```
# Create a new table
create_table_query = '''
CREATE TABLE IF NOT EXISTS users (
    id INTEGER PRIMARY KEY,
    username TEXT,
    email TEXT
);
'''
conn.execute(create_table_query)
```

3. Inserting Data:

Use the **INSERT INTO** statement to add data to the database.

```
# Insert data into the table
insert_query = "INSERT INTO users (username, email) VALUES (?, ?)"
data = ('john', 'john@example.com')
conn.execute(insert_query, data)
conn.commit()  # Commit changes
```

4. Retrieving Data:

You can use the **SELECT** statement to retrieve data from the database.

```
# Retrieve data from the table
```

```
select_query = "SELECT * FROM users"
result = conn.execute(select_query).fetchall()

for row in result:
    print(row)
```

5. Updating Data:

Use the **UPDATE** statement to modify existing data.

```
# Update data in the table
update_query = "UPDATE users SET email = ? WHERE username
= ?"
new_email = 'new_email@example.com'
conn.execute(update_query, (new_email, 'john'))
conn.commit()
```

6. Deleting Data:

To remove data from the database, use the **DELETE** statement.

```
# Delete data from the table
delete_query = "DELETE FROM users WHERE username = ?"
conn.execute(delete_query, ('john',))
conn.commit()
```

7. Closing the Connection:

Always close the database connection when you're done using it.

```
conn.close()
```

8. Using Context Managers:

You can use the **with** statement as a context manager to ensure the database connection is properly closed.

```
with sqlite3.connect('my_database.db') as conn:
    # Perform database operations within the context
```

9. Handling Errors:

When executing SQL statements, be prepared to handle exceptions, such as **sqlite3.IntegrityError** or **sqlite3.OperationalError**, that may occur due to data constraints or other issues.

Reading and writing data to databases is essential for managing structured information effectively. Whether you're storing user information, logs, or any other type of data, understanding SQL and utilizing Python's **sqlite3** module empowers you to interact with databases seamlessly. By following the steps outlined in this guide, you can insert, retrieve, update, and delete data from databases with confidence.

Developing a Simple Data Logging Application

A data logging application records and stores data over time, making it useful for various scenarios like monitoring sensor readings, tracking events, or maintaining records. We'll walk you through the process of developing a simple data logging application using Python and SQLite.

1. Set Up the Project:

Create a new directory for your project. Inside this directory, you'll create Python scripts to handle data logging.

2. Install Required Libraries:

You'll need the **sqlite3** module for working with SQLite databases. If you don't have it installed, you can install it using **pip**.

```
pip install sqlite3
```

3. Create the Database:

Create an SQLite database to store the logged data. You can do this using the **sqlite3** command-line tool or within your Python script.

```
import sqlite3

# Connect to the database or create a new one
conn = sqlite3.connect('data_log.db')

# Create a table to store data
create_table_query = '''
CREATE TABLE IF NOT EXISTS sensor_data (
    id INTEGER PRIMARY KEY,
    timestamp TIMESTAMP DEFAULT CURRENT_TIMESTAMP,
    value REAL
);
'''
conn.execute(create_table_query)
conn.commit()

# Close the connection
conn.close()
```

4. Logging Data:

Write a Python script to log data into the database. In this example, let's simulate sensor readings and log them into the database.

```python
import sqlite3
import random
import time

def log_data(value):
    conn = sqlite3.connect('data_log.db')
    insert_query = "INSERT INTO sensor_data (value) VALUES (?)"
    conn.execute(insert_query, (value,))
    conn.commit()
    conn.close()

while True:
    # Simulate sensor data (replace with real sensor reading)
    sensor_value = random.uniform(0, 100)
    log_data(sensor_value)
    print(f"Logged data: {sensor_value}")
    time.sleep(5)  # Log data every 5 seconds
```

5. Retrieving Data:

You can create another script to retrieve and display the logged data.

```python
import sqlite3

def retrieve_data():
    conn = sqlite3.connect('data_log.db')
    select_query = "SELECT timestamp, value FROM sensor_data"
    result = conn.execute(select_query).fetchall()
    conn.close()
    return result

data = retrieve_data()

for entry in data:
    timestamp, value = entry
    print(f"Timestamp: {timestamp}, Value: {value}")
```

6. Running the Application:

Run the data logging script to start logging simulated sensor data. Run the data retrieval script to see the logged data.

7. Enhancements:

- Modify the logging script to use real sensor data if you have a sensor connected to your Raspberry Pi.

- Implement error handling to deal with database errors or exceptions.

- Enhance data retrieval by adding filters, sorting, or aggregation features.

- Use a visualization library like Matplotlib to create graphs from the logged data.

Developing a simple data logging application allows you to record and manage data effectively. By using Python and SQLite, you can easily set up a database, log data, and retrieve it for analysis. This example serves as a foundation that you can build upon to create more sophisticated data logging applications tailored to your specific needs.

ADVANCED TOPICS AND PROJECTS

Introduction to Object-Oriented Programming (OOP)

Object-Oriented Programming (OOP) is a programming paradigm that models real-world entities as objects, allowing for more organized, modular, and maintainable code. It revolutionized software development by introducing the concept of bundling data (attributes) and the operations (methods) that manipulate that data into a single unit called an "object." Here's a comprehensive introduction to the key concepts of OOP:

1. Objects and Classes:

- **Object**: An object is an instance of a class. It represents a real-world entity and contains both data (attributes) and methods to operate on that data.

- **Class**: A class is a blueprint or template that defines the structure and behavior of objects. It encapsulates attributes and methods that are common to a group of objects.

2. Four Pillars of OOP:

OOP is built upon four fundamental principles:

- **Encapsulation**: Encapsulation refers to the bundling of data and methods that operate on that data within a single unit, the object. It hides the internal details of how an object works, exposing only what's necessary for the object to be used.

- **Abstraction**: Abstraction involves simplifying complex reality by modeling classes based on relevant attributes and behaviors. It allows you to focus on essential features and ignore irrelevant details.

- **Inheritance**: Inheritance allows a new class (subclass or derived class) to inherit properties and methods from an existing class (superclass or base class). This promotes code reuse and supports the creation of more specialized classes.

- **Polymorphism**: Polymorphism enables objects of different classes to be treated as instances of a common superclass. It allows for flexibility by allowing different classes to be used interchangeably when appropriate.

3. Attributes and Methods:

- **Attributes (Properties)**: Attributes are the data that objects hold. They represent characteristics or states of objects. For example, in a "Car" class, attributes could include "color," "make," and "model."

- **Methods (Functions)**: Methods are functions associated with objects. They define the operations that can be performed on objects. For example, in the "Car" class, methods could include "start_engine" and "accelerate."

4. Creating Objects:

To create an object in an OOP language (like Python, Java, or C++), you instantiate a class by calling its constructor method. This creates a new instance of the class (an object).

5. Real-World Analogy:

Think of a class as a blueprint for a house. The blueprint defines the structure and layout of the house (attributes), as well as the functions it can perform, like opening doors or turning on lights (methods). Actual houses built from that blueprint are instances (objects) of the class.

6. Benefits of OOP:

OOP offers numerous advantages, including:

- **Modularity**: Code is organized into self-contained objects, making it easier to manage and maintain.
- **Reusability**: Classes and objects can be reused in different parts of a program or in different programs.
- **Flexibility**: Changes made to one part of a program won't affect other parts, as long as the interface remains unchanged.
- **Scalability**: OOP principles facilitate building complex systems by breaking them into smaller, manageable components.

7. OOP in Practice:

OOP is widely used in software development for creating applications of various sizes and complexity. It's particularly effective for building GUI applications, games, web applications, and more.

Object-Oriented Programming revolutionized the way software is designed, written, and maintained by introducing the concept of objects, classes, and their interactions. By encapsulating data and behavior into objects, OOP promotes code organization, reusability, and modularity, leading to more robust and maintainable software systems. Understanding the principles of OOP is a crucial step toward becoming a proficient programmer in many modern programming languages.

Using Classes and Objects in Python

Classes and objects are at the core of object-oriented programming (OOP) in Python. They allow you to model real-world entities and encapsulate data and behavior into organized units.

1. Defining a Class:

To define a class in Python, use the **class** keyword followed by the class name. Inside the class, you can define attributes and methods.

```
class Dog:
    def __init__(self, name, age):
        self.name = name
        self.age = age

    def bark(self):
        print(f"{self.name} is barking!")
```

2. Creating Objects:

To create an object from a class, use the class name followed by parentheses. The **__init__()** method (constructor) is called to initialize the object's attributes.

```
dog1 = Dog("Buddy", 3)
dog2 = Dog("Luna", 2)
```

3. Accessing Attributes and Methods:

You can access attributes and methods of an object using dot notation.

```
print(dog1.name) # Output: Buddy
print(dog2.age)  # Output: 2

dog1.bark()    # Output: Buddy is barking!
```

4. Class Variables and Methods:

Class variables are shared among all instances of a class. They are defined inside the class but outside any methods.

```
class Circle:
   pi = 3.14159  # Class variable

   def __init__(self, radius):
      self.radius = radius

   def area(self):
      return self.pi * self.radius ** 2
```

5. Inheritance:

Inheritance allows you to create a new class (subclass) that inherits attributes and methods from an existing class (superclass).

```
class GoldenRetriever(Dog):
    def fetch(self):
        print(f"{self.name} is fetching the ball!")
```

6. Overriding Methods:

Subclasses can override methods from the superclass by providing their own implementation.

```
class Poodle(Dog):
    def bark(self):
        print(f"{self.name} is barking softly.")
```

7. Using Constructors:

The __init__() method is a constructor that initializes object attributes. It's automatically called when an object is created.

8. Private and Protected Attributes:

In Python, attributes can be marked as private (by using a leading underscore) or protected (by using a leading double underscore).

```
class Person:
    def __init__(self, name, age):
        self._name = name      # Protected attribute
        self.__age = age       # Private attribute
```

9. Dunder Methods (Magic Methods):

Dunder methods are special methods in Python that start and end with double underscores. They provide built-in functionality to classes, such as __str__(), __eq__(), and __len__().

10. Object Comparison:

Dunder method **__eq__()** allows you to define how objects of a class should be compared.

11. Using @classmethod and @staticmethod:

The **@classmethod** decorator allows you to define methods that operate on the class rather than instances. The **@staticmethod** decorator defines methods that don't require access to instance attributes or class attributes.

12. Property Decorators:

Property decorators allow you to define methods that behave like attributes, providing controlled access to attributes.

Using classes and objects in Python enables you to create organized and modular code by encapsulating data and behavior. Understanding how to define classes, create objects, and utilize inheritance and other OOP principles empowers you to build complex and maintainable software systems.

Exploring Machine Learning on Raspberry Pi

Machine learning, a subset of artificial intelligence, empowers computers to learn from data and make decisions or predictions without explicit programming. Raspberry Pi, a versatile and affordable single-board computer, can be a powerful platform for exploring and experimenting with machine learning. Here's a guide to get you started on exploring machine learning on Raspberry Pi:

1. Setting Up Raspberry Pi:

Ensure you have a Raspberry Pi board, an SD card with a

compatible operating system (like Raspberry Pi OS), and necessary peripherals (keyboard, mouse, display). You can also use headless setups and remote access tools.

2. Installing Python Libraries:

Python is a popular language for machine learning. Install libraries like **numpy**, **scikit-learn**, and **tensorflow** to work with data manipulation, machine learning algorithms, and deep learning models.

```
pip install numpy scikit-learn tensorflow
```

3. Machine Learning Basics:

Understand foundational concepts like supervised and unsupervised learning, training and testing data, features, labels, and model evaluation.

4. Simple Machine Learning Example:

Create a simple machine learning project on your Raspberry Pi. For instance, build a classifier to identify handwritten digits using the MNIST dataset.

```
import numpy as np
from sklearn.datasets import load_digits
from sklearn.model_selection import train_test_split
from sklearn.neighbors import KNeighborsClassifier

# Load the dataset
digits = load_digits()

# Split data into training and testing sets
X_train, X_test, y_train, y_test = train_test_split(digits.data,
```

```
digits.target, test_size=0.2)

# Create and train a k-nearest neighbors classifier
clf = KNeighborsClassifier(n_neighbors=3)
clf.fit(X_train, y_train)

# Evaluate the classifier
accuracy = clf.score(X_test, y_test)
print(f"Accuracy: {accuracy:.2f}")
```

5. Image Classification with TensorFlow:

TensorFlow is a powerful library for deep learning. Experiment with image classification using pre-trained models like MobileNet and TensorFlow Lite on Raspberry Pi's CPU or GPU (if available).

6. Object Detection:

Explore object detection using deep learning models like YOLO (You Only Look Once) to identify objects in images or even in real-time using the Raspberry Pi camera module.

7. Natural Language Processing (NLP):

Raspberry Pi can also handle natural language processing tasks. Use libraries like **NLTK** or **spaCy** for tasks like text classification, sentiment analysis, or chatbots.

8. Edge AI with Coral USB Accelerator:

Google's Coral USB Accelerator provides hardware acceleration for machine learning models. It's compatible with Raspberry Pi and can significantly speed up inference for models like image classification.

9. IoT and ML Integration:

Combine Raspberry Pi's capabilities with IoT projects. For

example, create a system that uses machine learning to analyze sensor data from a weather station or a home security setup.

10. Project Showcase:

Choose a specific machine learning project that excites you. Showcase your work through blog posts, videos, or GitHub repositories to share your experience and inspire others.

11. Learning Resources:

Utilize online tutorials, courses, and resources to deepen your understanding of machine learning and its applications on Raspberry Pi.

12. Community Engagement:

Participate in online forums and communities to ask questions, share your projects, and learn from others' experiences.

Exploring machine learning on Raspberry Pi offers a hands-on way to delve into the exciting field of AI. With the right tools, libraries, and a bit of creativity, you can build and experiment with a variety of machine learning projects right from your Raspberry Pi. Whether it's image classification, object detection, or natural language processing, the combination of Raspberry Pi's hardware and machine learning capabilities opens up a world of possibilities for learning and innovation.

TROUBLESHOOTING AND OPTIMIZATION

Debugging Techniques for Python on Raspberry Pi

Debugging is a critical skill for any programmer, and it becomes especially important when working with Python on a Raspberry Pi. Debugging helps identify and fix errors in your code, ensuring that your projects run smoothly.

1. Use Print Statements:

One of the simplest and effective debugging techniques is adding print statements to your code. Print statements help you understand the flow of your program and the values of variables at different points.

```
print("Debugging point 1")
variable = 42
print("Variable:", variable)
```

2. Check Indentation:

Python relies on proper indentation to define code blocks. Indentation errors can lead to unexpected behavior. Use consistent and correct indentation to avoid issues.

3. Utilize the Interactive Shell:

Python's interactive shell allows you to test code snippets and experiment in real-time. Launch the Python interpreter by typing **python** in the terminal. You can quickly try out code to understand its behavior.

4. Try Jupyter Notebooks:

Jupyter Notebooks provide an interactive environment where you can write and execute Python code in cells. They are useful for experimenting, debugging, and documenting your code step by step.

5. Use a Debugger:

Python offers built-in debugging tools. You can use the **pdb** module for interactive debugging. Place the following line where you want to set a breakpoint:

```
import pdb; pdb.set_trace()
```

When your code reaches this line, it will pause, and you can use commands like **n** (next), **c** (continue), and **p** (print) to inspect variables and step through the code.

6. Logging:

Instead of printing messages, you can use Python's **logging** module to log messages with different levels of severity. This helps you track the execution flow and identify issues without altering your code.

7. Exception Handling:

Use **try** and **except** blocks to handle exceptions gracefully. Catching and handling exceptions can prevent your program from crashing and provide insights into what went wrong.

```
try:
    result = 10 / 0
except ZeroDivisionError:
    print("Error: Division by zero")
```

8. Analyze Error Messages:

When an error occurs, Python provides error messages that describe the issue and often include the line number where the error occurred. Analyze these messages to pinpoint the source of the problem.

9. Divide and Conquer:

If you encounter a bug in a large codebase, divide the problem into smaller parts and test them individually. Isolating the problematic code makes debugging more manageable.

10. Rubber Duck Debugging:

Explaining your code or the problem you're facing to someone else (even an inanimate object like a rubber duck) can help you identify the issue. This process forces you to verbalize your thoughts and often leads to insights.

11. Revert to a Known State:

If you're unsure about changes that caused a bug, revert your code to a previously known working state using version control systems like Git.

12. Document Your Steps:

While debugging, document the steps you've taken and the solutions you've tried. This can save time if you encounter a similar issue in the future.

13. Review Your Code:

Review your code with a fresh perspective. Sometimes, the issue may be a simple oversight that you've repeatedly missed.

14. Community and Online Resources:

If you're stuck, don't hesitate to seek help from online communities, forums, or social media. Others might have encountered similar issues and can provide insights.

Debugging is an integral part of the programming process. By using a combination of techniques like print statements, debugging tools, exception handling, and careful analysis of error messages, you can efficiently identify and fix issues in your Python code on the Raspberry Pi. Becoming proficient at debugging not only helps you develop robust projects but also enhances your problem-solving skills as a programmer.

Optimizing Code for Better Performance

Optimizing code for improved performance is a crucial aspect of software development. Whether you're working on a large-scale application or a small script, efficient code can lead to faster execution, reduced resource consumption, and a better user experience.

1. Measure First:

Before optimizing, identify the specific parts of your code that need improvement. Use profiling tools to measure the execution time of different functions or sections. This data will guide your optimization efforts.

2. Choose Efficient Algorithms and Data Structures:

Optimize the efficiency of your code by selecting appropriate algorithms and data structures. Use algorithms with lower time complexity and choose data structures that provide efficient access and manipulation.

3. Reduce Redundant Work:

Avoid performing the same calculations or operations multiple times. Store results in variables if they are reused, and refactor code to eliminate redundant computations.

4. Minimize I/O Operations:

Input and output (I/O) operations are usually slower than computations. Minimize the number of I/O operations by reading or writing data in larger chunks and avoiding unnecessary file reads or writes.

5. Use Built-in Functions and Libraries:

Leverage built-in functions and standard libraries. They are often optimized for performance and can provide better results than custom implementations.

6. Avoid Global Variables:

Minimize the use of global variables, as accessing them can be slower than accessing local variables. Local variables are usually stored in registers or closer memory locations, leading to faster access times.

7. Loop Optimization:

Loops can be performance bottlenecks. Optimize loops by:

- Minimizing the number of iterations.
- Moving invariant calculations outside the loop.
- Using appropriate loop structures (**for** vs. **while**).

8. Memory Management:

Efficient memory usage can significantly impact performance. Avoid memory leaks by deallocating resources properly, and minimize memory fragmentation by reusing memory when possible.

9. Parallelism and Concurrency:

Explore options for parallelism and concurrency to take advantage of multi-core processors. Use libraries like **multiprocessing** in Python to parallelize tasks that can run simultaneously.

10. Caching:

Cache frequently used or computed data to avoid recomputation. Use techniques like memoization to store results of expensive function calls.

11. Profile and Analyze:

Use profiling tools to identify bottlenecks and performance issues. Profilers help you understand which parts of your code consume the most time and resources.

12. Micro-Optimizations:

Consider micro-optimizations (small changes that lead to minor improvements) only after addressing larger performance issues.

Micro-optimizations can sometimes make code less readable and maintainable.

13. Consider Trade-offs:

Optimization often involves trade-offs. Faster code might consume more memory, or a more memory-efficient approach might lead to slower execution. Consider the context and requirements of your project.

14. Benchmarking:

Benchmark your optimized code against the original to ensure that improvements are significant. Benchmarks help you validate the effectiveness of your optimization efforts.

15. Document Optimizations:

Document your optimization choices, especially if they involve non-standard practices or trade-offs. Clear documentation helps others understand your code and the reasoning behind optimizations.

16. Test Thoroughly:

Optimizations can introduce new bugs. Test your code thoroughly after making changes to ensure that it still works correctly.

17. Iterative Approach:

Optimization is often an iterative process. Continuously monitor and analyze your code's performance, and be prepared to revisit and refine your optimizations as the project evolves.

Optimizing code for better performance requires a balance between efficient algorithms, smart data structures, and careful coding practices. By measuring, analyzing, and applying optimization techniques, you can create software that runs faster, uses fewer resources, and provides an improved user experience. Remember that optimization is not a one-time task; it's an ongoing process that should be aligned with the specific needs and goals of your project.

Managing Resources and Memory Usage

Effective management of resources and memory is vital for creating efficient and robust software. Poor resource management can lead to slow performance, crashes, and a negative user experience.

1. Understand Resource Management:

Resource management encompasses not only memory but also other system resources like CPU, disk I/O, network connections, and more. Efficiently managing these resources contributes to overall system stability and performance.

2. Minimize Memory Usage:

Excessive memory usage can slow down your application and even cause it to crash. Employ the following strategies to minimize memory usage:

- **Use Efficient Data Structures**: Choose data structures that optimize memory consumption. For example, using a **set** instead of a **list** for membership checks can reduce memory overhead.

- **Avoid Redundant Data**: Store only necessary data. Don't duplicate information or create unnecessary copies.

- **Release Unneeded Resources**: Explicitly release resources like memory, file handles, and network connections when they are no longer needed.

3. Use Lazy Loading:

Lazy loading is a technique where resources are loaded only when they're required, rather than all at once. This can help conserve memory and improve startup times.

4. Implement Garbage Collection:

Garbage collection automatically reclaims memory occupied by objects that are no longer in use. Most modern programming languages, including Python, have built-in garbage collection mechanisms.

5. Handle Large Data Sets:

When working with large data sets, consider techniques like pagination, streaming, or processing data in chunks to avoid loading the entire dataset into memory at once.

6. Optimize File Operations:

When dealing with files, use buffered I/O to reduce the number of disk reads and writes. Close files explicitly after using them to release resources.

7. Leverage Connection Pooling:

If your application uses database connections or network connections, use connection pooling to efficiently manage and reuse connections instead of opening a new one for every operation.

8. Monitor Resource Usage:

Use monitoring tools to track resource usage and identify potential bottlenecks or areas of improvement. Tools like performance profilers and monitoring dashboards can provide valuable insights.

9. Prioritize Performance:

Optimizing for performance often involves trade-offs. Prioritize optimizing critical sections of code that are frequently executed or are resource-intensive.

10. Benchmark and Test:

Benchmark your application to measure its performance under different conditions. This helps you identify areas that need improvement and validate the effectiveness of your resource management strategies.

11. Plan for Scalability:

Design your software with scalability in mind. As your application grows, its resource requirements will also increase. Ensure your resource management strategies can handle higher workloads.

12. Optimize Database Queries:

If your application interacts with databases, optimize your queries for efficiency. Use indexes, avoid unnecessary joins, and limit the amount of data retrieved.

13. Manage External Dependencies:

External libraries and APIs can consume resources. Be aware of the resource consumption of third-party dependencies and ensure they are used judiciously.

14. Consider Mobile and Embedded Systems:

When developing for mobile devices or embedded systems like Raspberry Pi, resource constraints are more pronounced. Optimize your code to work within these limitations.

15. Plan for Failure:

Resource management includes handling exceptions and errors gracefully. Implement error-handling mechanisms to prevent resource leaks and ensure the application can recover from failures.

Managing resources and memory usage is a crucial aspect of software development that impacts both performance and user experience. By implementing efficient data structures, practicing lazy loading, optimizing file operations, and monitoring resource usage, you can create software that operates smoothly, consumes fewer resources, and provides a positive user experience. Balancing resource optimization with functionality and usability is essential for building reliable and efficient software systems.

Common Pitfalls and How to Avoid Them

In the world of software development, pitfalls are challenges and mistakes that can lead to bugs, security vulnerabilities, and inefficiencies in your code. By understanding and avoiding these pitfalls, you can create more robust and reliable software.

1. Lack of Planning:

Not planning your project thoroughly can lead to disorganized code, missed requirements, and frequent changes. Start by defining clear goals, requirements, and a project timeline.

Avoid: Spend ample time on project planning. Create a detailed project scope, identify potential challenges, and plan for iterations and adjustments.

2. Ignoring Security:

Neglecting security measures can result in vulnerabilities that expose your application to attacks. Lack of input validation, insecure dependencies, and poor authentication are common security pitfalls.

Avoid: Implement proper input validation, sanitize user inputs, keep dependencies updated, and follow secure coding practices. Use authentication and authorization mechanisms to protect sensitive data.

3. Hardcoding Sensitive Information:

Hardcoding passwords, API keys, and other sensitive data directly in your code makes it susceptible to exposure. Storing sensitive information in plain text can lead to security breaches.

Avoid: Store sensitive information in environment variables or configuration files. Use encryption to protect sensitive data at rest and in transit.

4. Not Testing Thoroughly:

Insufficient testing can lead to undiscovered bugs and inconsistencies in your code. Relying solely on manual testing without automated tests can slow down development and introduce errors.

Avoid: Implement a combination of unit tests, integration tests, and end-to-end tests. Use test-driven development (TDD) to ensure code quality and catch issues early.

5. Overlooking Code Documentation:

Lack of documentation makes it difficult for others (and even your future self) to understand and maintain your code. Code that lacks proper comments and explanations can lead to confusion.

Avoid: Document your code thoroughly with comments, docstrings, and explanations of complex logic. Maintain a README file to provide an overview of your project.

6. Not Handling Errors Properly:

Ignoring or improperly handling errors can lead to crashes and unexpected behavior. Users encountering cryptic error messages may become frustrated.

Avoid: Implement robust error handling by using try-except blocks, logging errors, and providing user-friendly error messages. Make sure your application gracefully handles unexpected scenarios.

7. Tight Coupling:

Tightly coupled code makes it challenging to make changes or add new features. Changes in one part of the codebase can inadvertently affect other parts.

Avoid: Follow the principles of modular and object-oriented programming to reduce coupling. Use interfaces, abstractions, and design patterns to promote decoupling and maintainability.

8. Ignoring Performance Optimization:

Neglecting performance optimization can result in slow and resource-intensive applications. Poorly optimized code can frustrate users and lead to scalability issues.

Avoid: Regularly profile your code to identify performance bottlenecks. Optimize critical sections, use caching, and choose efficient algorithms and data structures.

9. Reinventing the Wheel:

Writing custom solutions for problems that have established solutions can waste time and lead to maintenance challenges. Not leveraging existing libraries and frameworks is a common pitfall.

Avoid: Before building from scratch, research existing libraries and frameworks that address your needs. Leverage open-source solutions and contribute back to the community if possible.

10. Not Considering User Experience:

Focusing solely on functionality without considering user experience can result in unfriendly interfaces and frustrated users.

Avoid: Prioritize user experience by conducting usability testing, incorporating user feedback, and creating intuitive and responsive interfaces.

Awareness of common pitfalls is crucial for building high-quality software. By planning carefully, prioritizing security, thoroughly testing, documenting your code, and following best practices, you can avoid these pitfalls and create software that is reliable, secure, and efficient. Continuously learning from mistakes and adapting your development process will lead to more successful and satisfying projects.

www.ingramcontent.com/pod-product-compliance
Lightning Source LLC
LaVergne TN
LVHW051245050326
832903LV00028B/2584